Insight Tarot

Stanislav Reshetnikov

Copyright © 2020 by Stanislav Reshetnikov

Library of Congress Control Number: 2020930566

All rights reserved. No part of this work may be reproduced or used in any form or by any means—graphic, electronic, or mechanical, including photocopying or information storage and retrieval systems—without written permission from the publisher.

The scanning, uploading, and distribution of this book or any part thereof via the Internet or any other means without the permission of the publisher is illegal and punishable by law. Please purchase only authorized editions and do not participate in or encourage the electronic piracy of copyrighted materials.

"Red Feather Mind Body Spirit" logo is a trademark of Schiffer Publishing, Ltd.
"Red Feather Mind Body Spirit Feather" logo is a registered trademark of Schiffer Publishing, Ltd.

Designed by Danielle D. Farmer
Cover design by Danielle D. Farmer
Russian–English translation by Ivan Kosmynin

Type set in Kuenstler165 BT/Desire/Hypatia Sans Pro

ISBN: 978-0-7643-6002-2
Printed in China
5 4 3 2

Published by Red Feather Mind, Body, Spirit
An imprint of Schiffer Publishing, Ltd.
4880 Lower Valley Road
Atglen, PA 19310
Phone: (610) 593-1777; Fax: (610) 593-2002
E-mail: Info@schifferbooks.com
Web: www.redfeathermbs.com

For our complete selection of fine books on this and related subjects, please visit our website at www.schifferbooks.com. You may also write for a free catalog.

Schiffer Publishing's titles are available at special discounts for bulk purchases for sales promotions or premiums. Special editions, including personalized covers, corporate imprints, and excerpts, can be created in large quantities for special needs. For more information, contact the publisher.

We are always looking for people to write books on new and related subjects. If you have an idea for a book, please contact us at proposals@schifferbooks.com.

Discover yourself.

Possess yourself.

There's much more to that than pain.

CONTENTS

Introduction 7

How to Work with Tarot Cards 11

Major Arcana 15

Minor Arcana 87
    The Wands 88
    The Cups 100
    The Swords 112
    The Pentacles 124

Court Cards 137
    Pages 138
    Knights 144
    Queens 152
    Kings 162

Conclusion 173

Introduction

Every human being has a necessity to find his immortal Soul . . . as if wanting to wake from a dream where he is totally determined by his previous role.

Every one of us carries the knowledge of multidimensionality and spiritual depth—it is the gift we all possess. The only problem is that access to it is blocked. Too many times we have been told who and what we should be: what "foolish" and "practical" are for us, where we should go and who we should become, and what we should relate to. We believed those telling us those things, and have sealed ourselves. And now life is identified with a social mask, a "persona"—kind of a tested, made-up pattern. It is comfortable, safe, and customary, but one day it becomes unbearably dull, then . . . depressing. Finally, life completely drains out. Then a human, so unbelievably complex and deep, flattens into a 2-D copy of a Divine Design he was once meant to be.

Untapped potential of the Soul inflicts suffering. It's useless to hide from this fact within a chosen level of comfort or beautiful, rational concepts; there are the same stories of material security, social debt, family, motherhood and fatherhood, public opinion, and others. For every unrevealed piece of Soul, for every unfulfilled talent, we shall be called to account.

Revelation of True Self: Is that our main purpose?

Some search for the Soul in special places when they return to their stories, dreams, and memories. It could be a child's room, a music schoolteacher's cabinet, a place of personal power, a grandfather's kitchen garden with a greenhouse and fruit trees that looks like paradise in our memories, or a street—that street where it is possible to meet one's Self. For others, the Soul reveals itself in people, in the sacrament of human intimacy, in a talk that changes one's life. Some touch it in an act of creation, and some develop magical perception of the world, distinguishing its symbolic messages.

But whatever the Soul is, the signs that point the way are our insights—spontaneous epiphanies producing a different vision of events. It's as if you've been presented with the keys to something precious, something that's been locked, and you barely remember its existence: a fragment of an everyday story, a brief complete thought, a sensation transmitted, a feeling described, an appeal to a fairy tale or a myth . . . This creates a new meaning that becomes life-giving.

Insight Tarot is dedicated to all who seek this enlightenment and who are not afraid to welcome it with heart.

I have always been a mirror,
always reflected right what people came with.

When they'd come with fortunes,
I was a magnifying glass; when they'd come with sorrows,
I was a shrinking one.
I was able to enlarge what feeds life, and decrease what drains it.

But now I know that the truth is different.
I shall reflect fortune that is hidden beneath sorrow.

How to Work with Tarot Cards

1. Only practice will make you a tarologist—no matter how much it scares you or how comfortable it is. If you choose the Tarot path, you need to begin consulting.

2. The future is flexible; it contains an indefinite number of scenarios. Tarot shows a potential line of events that are most probably at a current time point, on the basis of choices that the querent has made, his current state, mind, emotions, and intentions, etc. If a scenario is appealing to a person, he may think about how to stick to it; if it is not—then he may think about what to do to change it.

3. Assist your querent in correct formulation of a question. The question should be concrete and concise. It should contain time frames, if it deals with terms. The question should not imply "yes" or "no" answers, but rather "What is the possibility?" and "How likely is it?"; the yes/no questions cause the illusion of fatality and in fact exempt the querent from responsibility for his choice and life. It is recommended to avoid health questions; there are professionals in charge for health in another area of expertise.

4. Tarot as a mantic system is the most effective for questions about the past, the present, and the near future. The questions about the distant future can be addressed, but the answers will be much less accurate. The distant future is a summary of all our choices from now till then. Until choices are made, Tarot sees them as many equally possible outcomes and hence cannot give precise answers. The near future assumes a limited number of decision points and a more robust general line of the events that flow, which can be distinguished by Tarot more clearly.

5. Start with only one or two simple readings. If needed, Tarot can address any question with a single card. Also, don't be afraid to construct your own readings.

6. The keywords for every card should be learned by heart. It is not easy, but very helpful, especially when a tarologist has difficulties or is just stuck. Keep trusted manuals handy. However, Tarot is always much bigger than a text from a white book or any manual. The true

Tarot work is not limited to reading from crib sheets, but a creative comprehension of meanings of playing Arcana through associations and analogies. It is a projective approach where the Tarot and a tarologist becomes a mirror reflecting internal processes of a client, helping him reveal a true "charged" core of a problem and an internal resource for a better resolution.

7. If you don't understand the message of an Arcanum in its position in a reading for a particular question, and its direct literal meanings do not help either, try one of two options:

   a. Start with a literal description of what is seen on a card: ("Here we can see a suffering person...") or
   b. Try to close your eyes and sense the emotions that the card induces in you; you can even let a bodily impulse come through and turn into a kind of hint for a motion; try to describe it.

8. One of the best ways to develop your Tarot talents is to embrace your intuition. If you remember the meanings of the cards, it rids you of the fantasies and wishful thinking; besides, knowing the meanings is insurance for a case when you are stuck. But the Tarot magic suggests a mix of traditions with a personal intuitive feeling. Ask for a hint from the Source—in the most comprehensible form for the universal good—and accept the first thought that comes to your mind. The most important thing in reading a card is the first spontaneous reaction and impression.

9. Don't be fearful of making a mistake or to fear consciously telling a lie. Try to be frank. Every person has his Ego; tarologists are not excluded. Everybody wants to have more recognition and less criticism; hence a temptation to adjust consultation to a client's expectations. Every second we catch feedback from others (face expressions, voice, breath, body movements, etc.), and if we want to be liked, we turn on our "built-in" customer-oriented approach. So, imagine that a querent is somewhere else and not near. You only know his question and see the cards in front of you.

10. You are not an arbiter of destiny. You are not a magician. You are a master who knows how to read messages of the Tarot cards. Why this particular reading came out to a querent, you don't know. And you cannot in any way guarantee that this particular future is expecting him to be there in it. But you *are* responsible to truthfully perform your duty; namely—to recite the reading.

11. Don't frighten your querent. Don't present your messages too dramatically. Avoid emotional effect. It's important to remember that the aim of a tarologist is not self-affirmation, but consolation, support, and help in seeking resources. Even negative cards can be read as important experiences and have a transformational potential. Ask yourself: What can a querent rely on? Don't leave a person alone with the negative outcome. Give him a hint on a direction to take.

12. Remember that a querent comes to you mostly seeking advice on something important for him. Don't judge and don't depreciate (even on the inside) questions of a querent (even if he asks what ink color to choose to write a letter to his grandma). Respect a querent in the same manner as you would expect someone to treat *your* questions and problems. Even an intuitive feeling of your respect and attention will allow a person to trust, become more open, and formulate his question more precisely.

13. Avoid temptation to seem omniscient, because nobody knows everything.

> An angel to a God, frightened: "Oh my god, they've discovered one more trans=uranium element!"
>
> God to the angel, calmly: "Just add one more nonlinear term to the Genuine Equation of the United Field."
>
> —A. Podvodny

14. Don't be afraid to talk to a querent in a dialogue mode. Tell him a bit about the work format, about the System. Clarify his question; elaborate more on details. The more information you get from a client, the more meaningful and helpful a reading will be. Ask a querent about his sensations, his impression from this or that Arcanum, which you consider important in the reading. Talk to him—this is important.

15. Pick the right words that will be understood by a querent. If a person is ready to hear and understand the message with the necessity of a spiritual growth—excellent. But if the words "mission," "supreme self," or "karma" don't tell anything to him that helps, and what he needs is practical advice, you must adjust the reading. If your interpretation is vague and stilted, it will hardly help; rather, it will plunge a client into confusion.

16. Tarot consulting is an energy-consuming process; it has to be reimbursable. At the beginning it can be a symbolic cash payment (or an exchange of services); further on, the

price of your consultations shall transform; set a price you consider fair and comfortable for yourself.

17. Is it allowed to read for oneself? There are no limitations about this; everything said above can be applied to one's own reading. Nevertheless, when we read for ourselves, it is much harder to be as objective and unbiased as with reading for others, and personal desire to see what one wants to see can interfere with the interpretation of the cards. One way or another, our psyche takes care of the status quo, and it takes guts to make it see what it doesn't want to see or (believes that it) can't handle. Still, to read for oneself is a good practice! Working with Tarot for ourselves, we learn to use the right Word (Logos) and express what is happening inside. And the more we do that, the less remains of the unspoken and unexpressed (exactly those things that cause neuroses). Besides, discovering oneself through the Tarot Arcana, we inevitably drift the level of our unconscious, hidden forces ruling our destiny. Letting in the energy of archetypes into our life, we begin to relive its completeness and fullness.

Major Arcana

The Fool (0)

The Magician (1)

The High Priestess (2)

The Empress (3)

The Emperor (4)

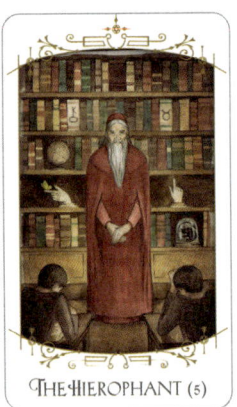
The Hierophant (5)

The Lovers (6)

The Chariot (7)

Justice (8)

The Hermit (9)

Wheel of Fortune (10)

Strength (11)

The Hanged Man (12)

Death (13)

Temperance (14)

The Devil (15)

The Tower (16)

The Star (17)

The Moon (18)

The Sun (19)

Judgement (20)
Resurrection

The World (21)

The White Card (–)

THE FOOL (0)

"The spirit of God moving over surface of the waters."
Zero point. Jump into the unknown. A space of variants.

I am the total potentiality. I can become anything.

An amazing Arcanum that has not seemed to have found a permanent place for itself. It moves between the start and the end, freely wandering over the deck, and seems to be able to replace any Arcanum. In a certain sense, the Tarot deck is a deck of one card—The Fool card. According to some interpretations he is a complete fool, who has forgotten about prudence; according to other ones, he is a higher spiritual entity free from material fears. Who is he?

I am the beginning of the Journey.

The Fool impersonates the hero, recklessly moving toward his destiny. But he is the one who gains The World at the end of his journey. He does not use the mind, but what is reckoned by a side observer as someone blind moving to a chasm, in fact, is a way to transformation so over the edge of this world that *brainiacs* can't even imagine it.

I am one of dreams of a sleeping god, dreaming about itself.

The Fool is the dwelling of soul before conception, when "Ego" hasn't been separated from The World yet. There are no borders between the outer and the inner, no self-consciousness, self-being—hence, no understanding of one's own possibilities or impossibilities, which gives absolute freedom. Freedom to be anyone.

He who wanders with no aim will never be lost.

Is there any order in these dreams, or does the deck shuffle itself all the time? Where there is The Fool, there isn't anything yet: zero—pre-beginning, primal integrity not lending itself for multiplication or division. There are no meanings, no predisposition. And at the same time there is everything undeveloped, in the bud—an infinite multitude of variants.

Stop being your own witness. Stop observing yourself. Do it without thinking.

The Fool requires you to dispose of the old experience, even the negative one. The experience just obstructs—on the basis of it, we build the frontiers of reality, losing the freedom of our own notions of it. The Fool, instead, ignites spontaneous creation not restricted by any previous experience or rules! Moreover, a person has no control over it, neither capable of keeping nor channeling to a certain direction.

I am a vagabond soul, cast to this world from a cosmic infinity.

The Fool means the period of stepping into the unknown—with a merry amusement and without any expectations, with a vast influx of energy. It is one of the cards of a wingman ("obeying the fate") of the uranic walking under God. The Fool doesn't emit well-being, alluring Ego. But it emits the kind of well-being of soul not tied to conditionalities, residing in a free journey, so as it should be in this world (according to Christ's word—"be passersby")

You can have anything with me—because it doesn't count.

UPRIGHT POSITION:

- Beginning of journey; a new impulse; a turn in a plot that no one expected
- Spontaneity, unpredictability, irrationality; originality, irregularity, absence of rules, laws, principles, borders
- Openness to all possibilities, curiosity, boldness, adventurism; completely new experience; trusting impulse
- Absence of greed and material ambitions; nonattachment

REVERSED POSITION:

- Chaos, disorder; unproved risks, irresponsible actions; fatalism
- Problems with spontaneity or creativity; absence of freedom and "internal approval"

The Magician (1)
Cocreator. Demiurge. Conjurer. Master.

I embody the energy called Consciousness.

The Magician is a God conceiving (birth of thought form, concept). There is nothing impossible for the Magician. If there is a goal, there will be a solution. Physiologically, the Magician represents human intelligence, this "beautiful mind," self-learning biological processor. Every second it creates new algorithms and protocols, establishing neuronal grids that resemble telecommunication grids—transmitting, receiving, analyzing information. An artificial intelligence is born . . . and it is The Magician too.

One needs to command only oneself, their own personal Universe of ideas and intentions.

Everything is energy, and, by thinking, we manage vast volumes of this energy in light and agile form—in the form of thought. A thought attempts to gain a form, trying to find its expression in an outer manifestation. A single thought does not possess a great power, but, being repeated multiple times, it can be concentrated and focused, significantly gaining power. Weak and scattered thoughts—weak and scattered powers. Strong and focused thoughts—strong and focused powers. The Magician is the epitome of faith in the power of mind and the power of positive thinking. Confidence in self, one's own powers and talents, can bring to life conscious mental energy, thanks to which fulfills the prophecy of self-realization—we become what we have imagined ourselves to be.

Think like every single thought is written in huge fiery letters in the sky.

Impersonated in The Magician, a man becomes a god's employee: he is the one who helps God comprehend itself. Endless intellectual abilities of The Magician is a mutual act of creation of God and human, a realized cocreation of The World—and this process should be utterly developed and responsible. The epiphany of the gift of The Magician appears on condition of excellence of our thoughts—when we understand that we obtain our ideas from the source much more sublime than our Ego.

A perfect instrument is interested neither in itself nor in performer or melody, but only in its own possibility to sound, play, and move forces of which it hasn't any idea, or to change the world because for a perfect instrument this is the very existence.

UPRIGHT POSITION:

- Idea or initiative, understanding of how it can be realized; precise action plan; project management
- Effective communication, eloquence, credibility; information access
- Consciousness, professionalism, dedication

REVERSED POSITION:

- Right idea evades mind; difficulties with seeking solutions
- Lack of self-confidence and faith in one's own potential
- Problems with communication and articulation of ideas
- The end justifies the means (hard-core manipulation, deceit)
- Unprofessionalism

The High Priestess (2)

Intuition. Hidden knowledge. Feminine aspect of God.

I'm married to mystery.

The High Priestess is the God disclosing (revelation of truth hidden inside). It impersonates women's wisdom (including in men) in mystical, magical, and metaphysical sense. Being imprisoned in material, The High Priestess belongs to the spiritual world. There is uncertainty, ambiguity of perspectives, and unclear future. It is the secret that will be unlocked in its time.

I can see through, read thoughts, and guess the past and the future.

The High Priestess is connected with the word "gnosis," which literally means "knowledge." But it's not a rational form of knowledge or studies with books; rather, it is a kind of knowledge gained through an intuitive comprehension of integrity. She means patience and readiness to hand oneself over to the supreme guidance, expecting that very moment when the awaited impulse appears.

The sea doesn't love anybody, but many feel happy near it.

It is considered to be a card of solitude, connected to personal austerity and mystical knowledge. In fact, The High Priestess doesn't really exclude relationships but instead points at weak predisposition toward their buildup. Its essence is an unlimited independence. Her responsibility about herself is very heavy, hence . . . self-sufficiency. And it's not a posture; it's the result of accepting herself.

An accidentally heard phrase can be the answer to your question.

Revelations and insights. Attention to knowledge and symbols. The responsibility of The High Priestess is incomprehensible events, mystical coincidences, various signs, which life sends us, and hints that the subconscious gives.

I acknowledge something is right only when I feel it's right.

UPRIGHT POSITION:

- Secret, mystery, hidden information, covert influence
- Intuition, premonition, unexplained irrational knowledge
- Wisdom, patience, tranquility

- Passiveness, "go with a flow," waiting position
- Introversion, privacy
- Advice of a wise woman, spiritual healing

REVERSED POSITION:

- The secret is revealed (or there is none; the question is about what is known already)
- Rejection or distortion of information (a knowledge about something)
- Bad contact with intuition, erroneous decision and judgments, unsuccessful attempts to rationalize
- Woman's solitude
- Negatively spirited elderly woman

THE EMPRESS (3)

Mother Nature. Wife and Lover. Abundant and Fertile. Loving and loved.

I am the divine feminine source accepting all and everything, bestowing flourishing.

The Empress encompasses four goddesses of the ancient Greek pantheon. There is Aphrodite in her, surrounded by the multitude of lovers, who coexists with Gera, fierce advocate of bonds of marriage and marital fidelity, and Demeter, who adores her children, merges together with Gaea, the goddess of Earth and mother to everything that lives and grows on it.

Your body is totally fine. Everything in you is beautiful. Just take off your clothes; let the partner enjoy your nuances.

If a man calls a woman "slut" or "greedy for money," in fact he wants to be adopted by her and is angry if he cannot do that. The adequate man will transform the anger into achievements and will compete with the other men. This is what the Empress assumes. All her rules are laid by the Nature.

In my womb there are all children who are to be born there.

She carries the fetus of future life, infinitely diverse in its manifestations. Behind the image of The Empress there is always the archetype of the Great Mother. Her impact on human destiny is immense. It is the mother figure, which during infancy determines perception of the world, feelings of basic safety, and acceptance or refusal by the world; it is she who establishes the feeling that everything is fine, the senses of affluence and sufficiency. Mother figure ignites in us that same self-value, which becomes vital source of love to oneself and the world. Because of that we can truly love someone only when we are fulfilled by the energy of The Empress. And it is she who can deny these states, making us greedily desire satisfaction and satiety in an effort to calm down anxiety . . .

I love you.

"Mom, mommy!"—this scream breaks out of our chest in the moments of catharsis. It is about the irreversible loss of the mother's womb paradise. All our life we search for the door leading back there. As it is written in Quran: Paradise is beneath your mother's feet.

UPRIGHT POSITION:

- Love
- Energy of life, growth and development, regeneration
- Affluence, fertility, generosity, care and grooming, safety
- Comfort, esthetics, taste
- Creativity
- Family, pregnancy, and birth
- Natural cyclic changes
- Mother, wife, housekeeper; particular woman—The Empress

REVERSED POSITION:

- Loss of life energy, stagnation, lack of inspiration
- Consumer attitude to environment and people, greed, cruelty
- Negation of one's own Empress
- Negative female models, including the mother's one (absent, not good, not loving, not caring)

The Emperor (4)

The father. The great organizer who won't allow chaos. Structure and order. Acts of will. The dyad of the Emperor and the Empress—God creator.

A real man is not who makes others do what he wants, but who makes himself do what has to be done.

The Emperor represents the father figure—it could be either a real father or just his imprinted image Contact with this archetype returns firm and competent behavior, confident and productive acts. Courage, persistence, pragmatism, logic, certainty, autonomy in decision-taking, ability to cope with life's challenges—all this is part of him. The Emperor persistently aspires for his goal. With this Arcanum comes the feeling of reality, the ability to create order in one's life and behave oneself with the emperor's dignity, not going soft.

Until you see me, you will know only uncertainty.

When internally positioned correctly, The Emperor becomes a reliable companion and protector. He also raises the question before a young man about his masculinity: How was it passed on to him by his father? What are the real means of self-fulfillment as a man?

This is my place. I am here justly and rightly. I am neither an impostor nor a scoundrel. I cannot be moved or devalued or canceled. This is my kingdom.

The Emperor is a creator, expressing himself through reclaiming the territory and designing it according to his own rules.

Put me in your center, and the fear of poverty will not oppose your opportunity to do your business.

The Emperor Arcanum embraces the questions of material stability and security related to the opportunity of becoming a master of one's own material life. He is the responsibility itself; to be aware of responsibility means to be aware of the fact that one's destiny is created by oneself. A man is what he becomes thanks to the business that he made his own.

I am the security and the safeguards. I'm invincible.

The Emperor carries in itself the figure 4, representing stability and basis. As with all quaternary structures, it is a reminder of the stability of creation and the sanctity of the divine plan. In spiritual questions it may mean the patriarchal figure of God as a father.

If I am inside you, you will never be a victim.

UPRIGHT POSITION:

- Expansion of the kingdom, determination, ambitions, social achievements, tangible result
- Power, authority, rational management, responsibility
- Structure and system
- Right decision
- Father, husband, boss, protector; particular man—"the Emperor"

REVERSED POSITION:

- Disruption of structure, loss of control and management, loss of power and influence; talentless decisions; rejection of responsibility
- Lack of discipline, gutlessness, spinelessness
- Stubbornness, rigidness, cruelty, abuse of power
- Negation or distortion of a male gender model, weak or absent or unfair father

The Hierophant (5)

Teacher. Mentor. Spiritual healer. Interpreter of the sacred.

I am the faith and the mode; my letter is "waw"—nail—just like a nail, the ideological rule staples structure and contiguity.

The Hierophant—God-educator.

I help follow the tradition, which grants dedication, study, and practices, leading to your own Grail. I am the people, the books, the canons and the rules, and spiritual systems helping neophytes. To walk the great road, one needs not only desire and intuition but also the wisdom of predecessors. I am this wisdom.

Experience of The Hierophant brings possibility to recognize in oneself, or in another person, what prevents evolution and what helps rectify it. He is a teacher from God. He has an angelic patience; he is never harsh. But the studies could be uneasy.

Never let yourself think that you have obtained the truth. Do not claim any knowledge. Don't formulate conclusions or estimations regarding verity. As soon as you imagine that you know something, you will cease to be open for a living study. You will close the door and cut off the oxygen supply for the truth to breathe.

The time has come to dust off such instruments as conscience—all of us regularly need that, even if we are decent people. But to follow one's conscience is hard: to live in conflict between the truth that the heart knows and the other one that we call "the truth of life." It is an incurable fifth wound of The Hierophant, and under his vestments he may be bleeding: how to follow the inner voice and to be righteous not only in fulfillment of one's purpose, but also toward oneself, and while listening to oneself, how to continue listening to the others. Our Ego center does everything it can to release us from evaluative pressure in these questions. When excessive, this pressure destroys, but its complete absence creates the same effect.

Practice what you preach.

UPRIGHT POSITION:

- Moral regulation of the system (habits, rules, ethical codices, commandments, dogmas, traditions)
- Religion and morality

- Wise advice, confidential talk, consultancy
- Education and mentorship, teaching, translation of knowledge
- Person of authority, mentor, consultant, priest, teacher, psychotherapist
- Voice of conscience

REVERSED POSITION:

- Bad advice (to or from someone, to oneself)
- Hypocrisy, imposed moral, condemnation; incompatibility of inner codices (ethical, moral, social)
- Disruption of studies (studies in direct and indirect senses)
- One-dimensional, close-minded vision, rigidity
- Rejection of traditional approach
- Manipulations, temptation, provocations; false prophet, black teacher

THE LOVERS (6)

Challenge of choice. Challenge of union.
Pursuit of unity and "common denominator."

I'm producing a desire to have what can belong to others.

The Lovers Arcanum reflects the stage of personal development when we realize that besides us there are others ("non-I"). Convergence fills up inner vacuum, returning sensations of integrity and meaning. We begin to understand that the others are similar to us and, for sure, not worse; learn to be in contact, interact, reach agreements, accept, yield, and trust. That's why The Lovers Arcanum is connected to building relationships of any kind: with partners, family, friends, colleagues, and even with the aspects of our own personality (for instance, with our desires). The Lovers help find common language and support unity and bonds.

If you want to drink—open up your palms; you can't scoop water with fists.

Our soul is a vast group of characters: part of them we sense in our identity, and others we find in surrounding people. So our contact, our proximity to the Other, is an attempt to achieve integrity of Soul. When falling in love with something, we believe that we find the most important meaning—that same missing part. But . . . "I like you because you have what I got used to considering sympathetic. And anywhere I look, I see only me. No one else is here." And the world around us is one big mirror reflecting our thoughts, wishes, and concerns. We all provoke each other to reflect one another. The difference is whether we can learn from what we see rather than take offense and turn away. Because seeing oneself in others is not easy; it's sometimes crucially hard and even disgusting.

Choose with your heart.

Is there freedom of choice? Or is that just an illusion, and, in reality, everything is determined by the past experience, social norms, and one's own projections? Regardless, The Lovers Arcanum puts us in a position to make a decision and the responsibility for the consequences of that decision.

You've grown up enough now, and so it's time to choose an angel to serve on the next segment of your Path. Who will you take along with you? What ideals will you let into your heart? Which goals will you set for yourself? Will you choose what you really want—or will your choices be predetermined by the dreams of your parents, opinions of surrounding people, fear—whoever or whatever, but not you? What will you sacrifice for your decision? No need to hurry with the answer, there is time to think. And choose.

UPRIGHT POSITION:

- Need to make a decision, choice; self-definition
- Establishing of relationships of any kind (including in the intermediary role), creation of liaisons, alliances, cooperation, partnership
- Romantic affair, crush, fascination with someone or something ("I like this," "I want this")

REVERSED POSITION:

- Imposed choice; uncertainty, doubts, delaying decision
- Insecurity, discord, adultery
- Problems with communication, misunderstanding, incompatibility, mistrust
- Codependency

The Chariot (7)

Victory of the free will. Action in the world. Triumph.

I am the center of a growing sphere. I intrude into the dimension where I am to reveal myself. I accept the challenge.

The hero of The Chariot is a young warrior, set to put the world to the test. He has separated from his parents' family, left the town of his father, and departed from the paradise of The Lovers Arcanum. He seems to be telling his parents: "I will prove that I'm worthy! Look at me! I'm an adult!" Whose hands keep and direct him? God's? Or maybe it is his mother's blessing—the one he's eager to be independent from so much? But the revolt against the unconscious may be the projection of the same unconscious.

I will combat everything that stands against me!

A person to whom The Chariot appears made the right choice on The Lovers Arcanum and now looks forward to his aim. Something familiar and habitual was left behind—he is creating a new reality, vigorously fertilizing space. Now he needs self-discipline and confidence in his intentions. He craves self-realization and self-improvement for the world to see.

I travel in time, not leaving the current moment. There is no past and no future. Only the present exists; everything is happening right here and nowhere else.

It is a stage of spiritual growth; the task is to learn to consciously manage different (sometimes controversial) impulses of one's own psyche, making them work together. The black horse and the white horse pull in different directions, but control of the operator provides synergy and progress to a common goal.

When I embody you, 10,000 reasons to reject something will not overcome one reason to continue.

The Chariot graciously allows you to be the helmsman. The main difficulty is to hold on to it and not to identify oneself with a God's chariot (as happened to Phaeton).

I am the action of the Universe itself.

UPRIGHT POSITION:

- Increase in dynamics of events, acceleration of processes
- Vigorous practical activity and energetic progress in business
- Achievement in any format
- Easy separation from the past, craving for the new
- Courage and readiness to risk; a right moment to be seized
- Optimism
- Self-control and discipline
- A trip

REVERSED POSITION:

- Wrongly chosen direction
- Halt, delay; hindrance, obstacles
- Loss of energy, fear to progress, fear to fail
- Loss of control over situation, escalation of chaos and misalignment

Justice (8)

A universal law. Regulation. Relevance of retribution to deed. Strictness and integrity.

I am neither good nor bad; I am the gatekeeper who restores the balance.

There is no justice in the human meaning of the word. But there is the balance among the elements of the system. Every one of us is such element—a member of a family, clan, society, organization, church, state, population, ethnos, and humankind. Everyone has relations with everyone and with the system as a whole. Everything is interconnected. Any action, thought, emotion of ours is imprinted in the Universe—and has its consequence, even though it's revealed ten minutes, ten days, or ten lives after.

What goes around—comes around.

The Arcanum Justice represents Karma principle—interconnection of actions and their consequences. Karma is an energy of retribution; its principle can be compared to a universal navigator, aiming a man through the reaction of the surrounding space, expressed through particular events and outcomes.

Of all the games, I prefer chess. First of all, everything is logical; second of all, everything is clear—it takes just a look around to see why things happened in this way and not the other.

The Arcanum does not define whether the acts are right or wrong; it solely states that the situation is of karmic nature (i.e., its predisposition lies in particular decisions and deeds). "Justice" is the Arcanum of personal responsibility, which requires working out debts and paying one's dues. An example of activation of this Arcanum is an attempt to solve a relatively easy task, which draws a plethora of unsolved and unaddressed earlier problems, probably, from different life spheres. "I will think of it tomorrow"—so, the tomorrow has come.

All rise; court is in session!

Coming in force of the energy of Justice is hardly pleasant. Any encounter of a person with the responsibility for his own actions does not carry anything bright for the Ego. Appearance of Justice means that one has to give a verdict to oneself, be objective about the reasons that provoked the situation, and accept responsibility for his own choice. The call of Justice creates an almost unbearable necessity to evaluate an event, a deed, an act. And to make that truly unbiased.

Everybody wants the truth to be on his side, but not everyone wants to be on the truth's side.

UPRIGHT POSITION:

- An encounter with a result of one's own deeds and decisions (a contact with the universal law of a cause and a consequence—with Karma)
- Adequate valuation, fair criticism, robust approach, well-thought-out decision
- Honesty and objectivity
- Equal partnerships
- Law norms, systems and procedures, legitimacy check, conclusion of contracts and agreements, invoices and payments; to act according to established rules
- Ruthlessness, intransigence

REVERSED POSITION:

- Attempt (senseless one) to avoid consequences of one's own deeds and decisions; negation of one's own association with consequences of one's own actions, belief in one's own infallibility
- Distortion of reality; misconceptions
- Problems with the law, infringements of rules and agreements
- Unfair situation, untruthful decision, bias

The Hermit (9)

Seclusion. Inner loneliness—without pain. Self=dedication.
Dark space where spiritual transformation takes place.

It is a desert, but here God speaks to me. Hence live in silence—to hear him.

A stage in spiritual development symbolizes self-absorption, a pullback from the world to a monastery of spirit. The Hermit leaves for the dark to find inner light. Basically, The Hermit looks for a purpose—a way it, in fact, should be.

I immerse my light into the dark waters of inner infinity.

The Mystery of this Arcanum is the quest for truth, existential contemplation, attainment of immaterial treasures, searching and getting answers in the inner world. Secluded, The Hermit accumulates and concentrates potential energies that shall become the basis for an alternative being in the future. It is a state of spiritual pregnancy.

The Hermit means faithfulness to one's own life principles, indifference to opinions and estimations of surrounding people and to conventional stereotypes of thinking and behavior.

Your main task now is to calm down any fuss and tantrum. To hear a new you. You are not sick, stressed, or fallen. You are transforming. This doesn't happen fast.

This period requires several things: total iron will, absolute discipline, absolute egoistic self-reflection. And on top of that, total public invisibility.

What you are looking for is looking for you too.

UPRIGHT POSITION:

- Thinking things over, introspection, analysis of past experience, revision of life values, "reboot"
- Wise, well-thought advice
- Individualism, autonomy, self-sufficiency
- Seclusion, isolation, loneliness
- Scrutiny, meticulousness, attention to details, mastery
- "Not warm"
- Elderly man ("iron Oldman")
- Sobriety, limitation, abstention, spiritual practices
- Will and discipline

REVERSED POSITION:

- Fear of loneliness, dependence on social interactions
- Low capability of self-analysis and introspection, superficiality
- Own ideas of cult, egoism, counterdependent narcissism
- Self-punishment in the name of a higher goal (exhausting diets, exercises, etc.)
- Misanthropy, asocial forms of behavior
- Introversion in its extreme form, social phobia

Wheel of Fortune (10)

Fate. Predisposition. Versatility. Fortune.

I achieved stability a countless number of times.

Wheel of Fortune speaks of inevitable change of ups and downs, prosperity and hardship, joy and sorrow. The symbol of this Arcanum is a wheel or a spiral twirling from the beginning till the end of times. What was brought up will be taken down on the next cycle. And what has fallen to the deepest point of existence will go up. Nothing is permanent, nothing is reliable, nothing exists as an immutable reality. "This too shall pass." . . . The dynamics of life shall be taken philosophically.

When God wants to remain unknown, it is called "an accident."

Some perceive Wheel of Fortune as "unfair," but it is another kind of "fair"—the bills are calculated on such a level that we just can't understand how to match cause and effect. What takes place under the Wheel of Fortune seems to be an accident—a happy or a fatal one—but in reality there is nothing accidental. Epitomizing the very Fate, the Wheel of Fortune has the power of karmic dimensions, which seems incomprehensible to us, and that includes the extension of the fate of something bigger to which a man belongs.

You don't have to do anything—just fasten your seat belts, breath out, and relax . . .

There are many cards among the Major Arcana of Tarot that proclaim the coming of a tipping point. It makes sense—any evolution happens only through crises, through change. But each Arcanum emphasizes each kind of change. The Wheel of Fortune also has its own taste: it is the Arcanum of unexpected changes (surprises), but these changes are fortunate (even if scary at the beginning). It is Kyros—that very right moment when nothing special was ever expected and—boom!—it happens.

Everything that happens is your destiny; moreover, it smiles at you.

UPRIGHT POSITION:

- Unexpected fateful situations (with a feeling of losing control over what happens); luck; opportunities
- End of a previous cycle, beginning of a new one; transition to a new level
- "Uncalculated factor"
- Optimism and adventurism
- Circulation of events

REVERSED POSITION:

- Repeated situation (returning to the starting point)
- Resistance to changes, fear to risk
- Inappropriate moment

Strength (11)

Condescend to Beast, releasing its origin in self. Instinctive vitality. Intuitive order and will, transforming wilderness into art.

I feel and accept all of me. I am aware of myself from head to toe. I breathe out wishes.

The Strength card brings us to underlying animal instincts—as a rule, socially unacceptable; at the same time, they are the sources of primal vital power. This Arcanum is about their acceptance and how to treat them. Don't kill, don't torture, don't punish, don't deny. Accept, respect, sense, name their needs, find sustainable solution for their satisfaction. Be the owner of your own instincts—not through tyranny, but via the spirit strength, order, and love to one's own passionate animal origin and its bodily intuition.

> *It will be it as you wish.*
> *And it is as you wish.*
> *And it was as you wished.*

It is an archaic African fairy tale, a work with energies—through breath, motion, and sound. It is purification of the body and its filling. It is traditions of Kundalini and juxtaposition with the archetype of Shakti—the Great Mother in her warrior persona. Women can beg her for protection—inspiration of power, resilience, and victory over enemies. She is a feminist and protector of all her daughters. Although women often don't realize all their abilities, psychic strength of a woman is immense. The power of her sexual energy can do anything. It is a feminine individuation, discovery, and ownership of new parts of herself, including rage and fury . . . including rage toward her mother—and acquisition of her own woman's strength through that.

Become the top dog of the pack. Primarily of the pack that is in you.

The Strength is a power with a certain vector. Strength transforms chaos and builds Order. Order is when everything is used according to its purpose—supremacy of higher vibrations over lower ones without any coercion, just due to their nature. Their presence is just enough. When there is natural inner strength, the necessity to apply outer strength is minimal.

Wild energies take shape inside me.

UPRIGHT POSITION:

- Strength of will, resilience, determination; ability to overcome difficulties; high productivity
- Ownership of situation, structuring and organization according to one's own will; backbone; interpersonal order; self-discipline
- Leadership, strenuousness, vehemence, stance
- Healthy sexuality, physical attraction, tantric sexual practices, conscious intimacy
- Physical power, stamina, immunity, robust health
- Comprehension and strengthening of the controlled bond "body-psyche"; corporal practices
- Female initiations, female leadership

REVERSED POSITION:

- Rejection or suppression of instincts and vital desires leads to physical degradation, fear, loss of will and self-confidence (weakness, powerlessness, distress, self-accusations, depression)
- Repressed anger and rage (subconsciously redirected toward oneself)
- Aggressiveness, inclination to repress and domination, "wild behavior," "beastly behavior," problems with self-control
- Chaos, disruption of order, unjustified transgressions

THE HANGED MAN (12)

Martyr. Choice without choice. Sacrifice of Ego. Wounded Healer.

I sacrifice.

Every one of us is walking up the hill. On this road we do good and bad things, accumulating merits and knowledge, trying to become better. When we are at the top, we see a cross. And everything that we created or acquired, the most valuable and precious, should be sacrificed. "Whatever I do makes it worse." And then, from defeat, helplessness and humility comes a new insight, a new vision of situation and oneself.

What has been left of me?

The Hanged Man is what happens to a person who has been bogged down with material worries and who rejects seeing what the Spirit—the next stage of evolution of the personality—requires of him. When the so-called real world is on halt, one receives the opportunity to understand it. When the will has tied the arms and legs, a chance to shift the "assembly point" appears. The Hanged Man weans to cling to "the face," control, power, conveniences, and attachments. It does not lecture like The Hierophant, does not call for objectivity like the Justice, and does not crush like The Tower. It just . . . hangs. Deprived of power and control, it presents the true humble readiness to accept changes.

The time has stopped for me. I'm immobilized, unable to change anything. I turned upside down and see the world accordingly. I see the hidden nature of things.

The Hanged Man hangs the situation so that the usual reaction models become totally obsolete. What we used to reckon to be right ceases to be beneficial and even becomes harmful. Instead, those things we previously turned down are useful now, but we can hardly utilize them or we are still afraid of them. We find ourselves in a position that is very uncomfortable and inconvenient for us—as we would be hanged upside down. Sensation of a forceful hanging and suspension deprives us of independence, but it can offer something new and precious if the right question is found. Experience shows that the question "Why did it happen to me?" is a dead-end one. But to question "Who am I that this has happened to me?" has a chance to reveal hidden treasures. But sometimes we substitute and make a false sacrifice. We demonstrate helplessness to benefit from it, using dependent conditions to manipulate circumstances and people around us. This way revelation never comes, and we continue to be stuck in a dead end, gloomily waiting for the end.

The more you try to hang on, the more is the probability that you fail.

UPRIGHT POSITION:

- Forced change in values; necessity to do something unpleasant, uncomfortable, shameful, humiliating, insulting; painful (and, as a rule, forced) transformation of one's own rules and predispositions; "feel oneself a victim"
- Crisis; hopeless situations and feeling of a dead end; helplessness; halt of processes; material loss; deterioration of health
- Agreement, resignation, acceptance; spiritual comprehension of the deeper sense of what is taking place; confession, spiritual practices, austerity

REVERSED POSITION:

- Resistance to "educational process," the lesson of The Hanged Man has not been learned, situation becomes worse
- Egoism, spiritual immaturity, and fixation on the material aspects

Death (13)

Between the past already gone and the future yet to come.
Transformation. Change of condition.

The Arcanum of the Death is not about physical death. Its territory is the death of self-definition, anachronistic part of one's own Ego identity. Death marks those places that were totally vacated by tension, just like the current from a power grid. Dead can become relationships, work, habits, environment, ideas, behavior models . . . Death is surrounded by the grief of loss and the pain of separation—but not only. It also carries relief because something that had exhausted itself fell off easily.

I am a God-given Shadow of Fertile Mother. Every one of you experienced an encounter with me. That was your birth. Don't be afraid of me. I won't do any harm to a living; instead I will clean up space from the wrecked, doomed things that do not bear any sense anymore.

Sorrow of irreplaceable loss and fear of the unknown. Fear of changes. But the time has come to grief, forgive, farewell, and let go.

Readiness for this loss, its acceptance, is also a part of the price. To find yourself in new relations—you have to get over the old ones. At least strip off from familiar and habitual solitude. To acquire a new position or a status, you have to lose your old condition. To become rich, you have to lose the inner position of a poor man. This is how we become adults.

Children cannot imagine me, because if they do, they will stop being children, for I am the end of the childhood . . .

The Death is the condition of possibility of changes. Shall we call it Time? Relentless Time is the measure of longevity of existence of all objects, the characteristic of change of their conditions. Irreversibility of time equals irreversibility of death: it continues only in one direction, from the past through the present into the future.

Let's try to die right now, permanently, irrevocably, and without any hope to heal.

UPRIGHT POSITION:

- Between the already gone past and the yet-to-come future—stage of slow irreversible changes; natural final of the previous phase
- Departure, separation, "letting go," mourning
- Transformation, conversion, vacation of space for the new
- Cycling of everyday life

REVERSED POSITION:

- Fear of change, resistance to changes, retention of the old and anachronistic
- Stagnation, rot, decay
- Long, pessimistic, with a loss of energy; depression
- "He's not dead! Not dead!" (hugging decaying corpse)

TEMPERANCE (14)

Integration of opposites. Art of balance and small steps.
Unity. Presence of compassionate power.

Don't wait till it turns easier, simpler, better. Learn to be happy right now—locally.

Are we able to enjoy everyday life and usual routines? Looking uncomplicated and simple, even boring, Temperance is one of the uneasiest Arcana. It seems to epitomize "nice and quiet," but the paradox is that its true meaning can be fathomed only in the very thick of durability test. The figure of this angel is distinguished not only by itself, but against a hellish glow incinerating life. To see it amid the ordinary is a precious skill, gained at high cost. We begin to cherish a measured pass of time only having survived through turbulences and loss.

I accept differences without splitting into the good and the bad.

The body seeks pleasures and safety, the soul—beauty and harmony, the spirit—Heaven and God. The art of Temperance consists of acceptance and reconciliation of this conflict. Annihilation of polar passions comes and the "middle path" of soul is born. Temperance is a great peacemaker, both external and internal.

I create the higher alchemy—making the space to restore inner circulation, to melt and rejoin on a new level what has been divided.

Who is this way? He is the other way too. He is not "truly" so; he is "at the same time" so. The real thing is real only when at the same time it is its opposite. A true lover cannot be true unless she is a true wife, and true man is true only when he is a woman at the same time.

There where the extremes converge—there is the truth.

Temperance supports in physical and spiritual life. The Arcanum is of healing both psychic and physical; purification of body and soul through contemplation and abstention from unnecessary actions and thoughts. Temperance does not calm down; rather, it wakes up to a completely new level of understanding, and it's not a dead point. It says about establishment of control over one's own life thanks to a conscious choice and not because of tossing between the rival poles.

I am your Guardian Angel.

UPRIGHT POSITION:

- Conflict resolution, reconciliation, elimination of contradictions, consolation
- Inner balance, patience, calm
- Peacekeeping, diplomacy
- Modesty, sense of proportion
- To be satisfied with little
- Healing, sanitation (including getting rid of the dependencies)
- Punctuality, accuracy, prudence, attention to details
- Routine, monotony, slow pace of time

REVERSED POSITION:

- Loss of stability and regularity
- Imbalances, immoderation, anxiety, impulsivity, difficulties with self-control
- Lack of mutual understanding, problems with adaptation
- Nervous meltdowns, mood swings, loss of energy
- Excessive conformism

THE DEVIL (15)

The dark side of the power. Obsession.
Dependencies. The Shadow.

My main trick is to pretend that I don't exist.

We live in a world where there is light and shadow, the good and the evil. And how is the evil inside us going? Do we know the "true" self? Meeting our darkness, we react differently: with a protest, negation, arrogance, self-flagellation. We assign devilish traits to what we don't want to see—what we leave behind the scene of our consciousness.

I'm allowed to do anything. I'm better than others. If that brings me pleasure, the rest must tolerate. No one dares to disapprove of me.

The Devil is an archetypical antagonist, religious-mythologic personification of Evil. He is a seducer, provoking manifestations of human viciousness, aiming to divert a man from God. And the easiest trap to fall into is pride.

"Just kill him. Everybody here does so."

We cannot see our own Devil—he is hidden in the shadow of our psyche. These are the hands of an invisible puppet master—the ruler of the material world. Countless rationalizations are made up by our ego so that we do not acknowledge his power over us. "How could it be Devil at all? It's called career growth!" ... "These are just the rules of survival in a big city!" ... "It's just a beneficial decision!". ... "I'm doing it with the best intentions!" ...

You have the master.

A person is captured by some compulsive idea, fear, or any imperative impulse with a destructive potential. It is a stage in spiritual evolution, symbolizing collision with darker aspects of one's own personality, that subtly controls us. It is an examination over the period of which one can face the involutional part of one's nature, which has been kept unaccepted or, even if accepted with open arms, can't be controlled. The Devil can mean dependency on habits, pleasures—and sometimes dependency on another person.

Sanctity is also a temptation.

Diabolos—the one who divides. We blame ourselves and others, suffer from resentments, get annoyed by other people, consider it inconvenient and inappropriate to voice our necessities, fight for justice, sacrifice ourselves—because it is so important for us to stay good in our own eyes. "I want to be good! I don't want to destroy!" Alas. Those who want to live and not to destroy—don't live. It can be dislodged, any conflict situation can be avoided, negative feelings can be contained, but it's impossible to be yourself without disturbing others. Life requires one to make mistakes, villainies, to lie and be deceived. To be weak, dependent. To betray. All of this is to be included in the bill! Otherwise, it's about filling oneself up with a special liquid and placing it into a museum, just like an artifact. To draw a plate according to one's ideal fantasies about self—"a good boy" or "a good girl."

If you witnessed what you contain, then what you witnessed will save you. If you reject what you contain, then what you rejected will ruin you.

UPRIGHT POSITION:

- Dependency on another person, habits, material values, sex, food, alcohol, drugs, etc.
- Exploitation of the resource of space and other people to satisfy one's own egoistic desires (aspiration for power, pleasures, manipulation, temptation, submission, sadism); feeling of total entitlement and absence of punishment
- Moral covenants; collision with a shadow part of personality; something that makes one feel ashamed
- Violation of social rules, laws, norms, morale, taboos; forbidden pleasures and temptations
- Big money, but the price is to compromise on principles
- Wild party, Sabbath, orgy

REVERSED POSITION:

- Awareness of dependency and capture; attempt to break free
- Painful acceptance of one's own shadow traits, inner transformation
- Way out of an unpleasant situation through acknowledgment and disclosure of the truth

The Tower (16)

Purification by the flame. Catharsis that brings liberation. Entering the future with the rumble of the present.

It is not pleasant to be treated as a child who's being dragged to a dentist to remove a bad tooth. Hardly anyone is delighted to expect such operations; nevertheless they are necessary.

The Tower is the outcome of loss of connection with one's own spiritual center, adaptation of restricting forms, placing oneself into the narrowness of The Tower (by putting on the crown of one's own wrongness). Our subconscious activates this archetype when we are stuck in "the prison of our head," in the stable structures of our fears, stereotypes, and life attitudes. If we are unable to accept necessity of changes and break down lifeless artificial limits—then The Tower does it for us.

If my house is on fire—it means God is knocking at my door.

This Arcanum contains much energy of anger. It is the anger of our higher self. It is outraged and is waking up to dispel illusion. The Tower shows that the walls behind which we were hiding in fact were our cage. It had locked our unused powers and opportunities, undisclosed emotions, unreleased desires. And now this energy is breaking out, crushing that hated prison.

I'm burning down the bridge you wanted to cross to return in the past.

The Tower symbolizes the end of current stagnant situations, both quick and unexpected.

I destroy only what is already dead and what has to be demolished.

With the assistance of The Tower, we clean up the garbage, throw away the old and unnecessary, and eliminate obstacles. The card says that we are inside a very intense process of transformation; something has shaken us up and over, we sensed an impulse for something important, and a place inside us has been cleared for something new. We relive shock and liberation.

Broke down the door and walked out.

Sometimes the Arcanum The Tower is a conflict and sometimes an uncontained sexual impulse. Sometimes one turns into the other . . . but in any case, it's an explosion and release of long-accumulated suppressed feelings. If something has been kept under a bushel, bridled, tolerated, silenced, waited, then The Tower is the hour of explosion. It symbolizes the mighty orgasmic power of emotions that were contained for a long time but finally were released.

Dead end is the perfect excuse to begin crushing the walls.

Upright position:

- Shock, sudden unwanted changes
- Release from the old
- Unexpectedly bright and "energetic" event, changing the format of customary perception
- Strong emotional reaction

Reversed position:

- Reluctance to imminent changes, attempts to patch up the hole, "a doorstop for a rotten house"; ignoring the necessity of radical changes
- A dead construct is still holding on but is about to fall down

The Star (17)

Guiding light. Hope. Dream. Anticipation of the future.

Don't destroy fruits of faith and you will harvest fruits of faith.

The Star Arcanum is intuitively comprehensive through the image of a star, universal for all cultures. A star could serve both as guidance and as a sign of a human destiny—hence the story of the star that shined as the sign of a birth of the messiah for the Three Kings, the Magi in the Christian legend.

If you see your dream—then your subconscious has already built a road to it.

We know that our Star exists. IT is a dream, a goal, which is set in front of our inner sight, a wish that is ready to be made at any fleeting moment ("until a star is falling"). It is faith and hope that live in our soul and sometimes are seen as sky-high fantasies. The Star reconfirms and blesses an intuitive belief of a person that he can live up to his highest dream, standing firmly on the ground at the same time.

We all are cosmic brothers, tied by invisible threads—energies, existing out of space and time.

Feeling small as a speck of dust in the infinite space, a spark among billions of stars, we, at the same time, sense our belonging to the processes of the universal scale. The Star reminds us that everything is interconnected. A fate of a man is no exclusion: it is closely, sophisticatedly, and unexplainably linked to destinies of other people.

Be like stars.

The Star is a symbol of Ineffable Beauty and a projection of our quest for what is impossible, but essential to obtain. It gives enormous, almost inexhaustible, possibilities for personal growth and development.

You feel presence of the highest guiding force you shall trust in.

Nobody will ever be lost for good—as soon as we ask our fortune for help, it comes to the rescue and shows the way. The Star is a guiding light of the spirit, which stayed with us after we survived devastating and painful shocks of The Tower that demolished our previous ego, obsolete values, and affections.

Love is to provide a space to the other for his soul to find its way.

Upright position:

- Seeking new landmarks and high goals, principles and purpose of own actions, one's own mission in this life; distant perspectives
- Feeling of the right path; hope
- Inspiration
- Sustainability
- Platonic feelings

Reversed position:

- Loss of connection to the inner "navigator," lack of feeling that the chosen path is right, devastation, "nothing shines for me there"
- Disengagement from any material questions (including provision of basic needs)
- Fleeing to abstract contemplations; excessive, overly theoretical approach with no link to the practical side of a question
- "Starstruck," arrogance, keeping distance

The Moon (18)

Fragmentation of self=image. Illusions. Obsession. Naked perception. Creation of phantom worlds.

I'm falling into myself, deeper and deeper each time. I'm fragmenting, losing myself. I'm scary and provoke terror and unconscious melancholy. I've lost myself descending to nowhere until I ceased to exist.

Irrational behavior, drowning into the world of fantasies and reveries, walking on the edge. The Arcanum diverts into dreams and to all those special states of soul, related to the "lunar" (or "insane") nature. Inundating power of subconscious makes us unreliable, but at the same time it brings premonitions and great dreams in which we can identify with any form of life.

I'm a mire of immeasurable fortune. The more you step into me, the more I attract you.

An infinite potential of perception and sensitivity of the Moon is its greatest treasure. To enter such state of total perception, the Moon completely abandons giving back. Its fickle light is always a distorted reflection.

I am a universal mirror. Everyone can see himself in me.

"Unverified reports suggest that under unclear circumstances, . . ." The edge between precisely working intuition and the imagination that generates illusions is as blurred as ever. Either we mislead someone, or somebody misleads us, or we delude ourselves with something. Anxiety when there's no solid ground under your feet. What we feel under the Arcanum The Moon is separated from its meanings. A projecting consciousness creates phantom realities attributing qualities to outer objects, not even suspecting that it is the host and the source of that content.

You ask me to explain myself, but it's beyond my power.

Upright position:

- An outstanding situation, uncertainty
- Obsession, illusions, irrationality, disconnection from reality and facts, suggestibility
- Superstitions
- Lies, ambiguity
- Hazy feelings, sense of loss, anxiety, fears
- Intuitive insights, ominous dreams, increased sensitivity
- Altered states of consciousness, witchcraft, divination, shamanism, sorcery

- Alcoholism, drug addiction, mental illness
- Women's mysteries, women's magic

Reversed position:

- Exposed hoax, clarification of convoluted situations
- Illusions fade, delusions dissipate

The Sun (19)

Meeting your Inner child. Happiness. Internal source. Achieving intrinsic value.

There where I shine—all doubts vanish.

The Arcanum draws a picture of an immediate joy of life, total satisfaction with what it gives, and pleasure from its sunny, cloudless side. The Sun is the Arcanum of a childish, spontaneous perception. A talent to be happy here and now. Living through one's own authenticity and universality, integrity and unity with the whole loving world.

You are the best present to this world.

We are grown-up people continuing to stay children deep inside. Everybody has this memory and feeling from childhood—"that is when I was truly happy." We recall how everything greatly interested us, how we explored the space around us, always looking for adventures, and we would wake up expecting wonders to be coming our way. Thanks to the inner child we have curiosity and aspiration to the unknown. The other traits of our personality are quite conservative and wary about everything new, and only our inner child is always delighted at any unexpected turns in life. Such moments bring him anticipation of adventures, and those are what he is dreaming of. The Sun Arcanum is a state when the inner child is not kept locked but actively participates in the psychic life. When he is with us, we are spontaneous, free, and full of creative energy.

Ability to love oneself and take care of oneself does not fall from heaven—it forms as a result of care and love received from others.

Seems that those who are forged by hardship from their childhood will be better at handling it later on. It is not so. Better at handling difficulties are those who had a happy childhood and a good family. Their mental state has a safety margin, and, under stress, it continues to stay flexible and ingenious; they are not afraid to ask for help and, if needed, are able to console themselves. Those who suffered in their childhood and who had to deal with fear and pain without any help from their parents are very sensitive to stress, falling either into aggression or despair.

To have something to give, it first has to be received.

Every person needs to live for themselves—to activate their own Sun. To be the center of attention, to fill oneself with others' resources. It's crucial! Then the will to give back and share will appear. Until a person is complete, he or she can pretend to give back, to be a good employee, parent, or member of society. But he does not invest from excess; he gives back out of the need, tearing off from himself his precious scarce resource.

I don't know what "shame" is.

If we depend too much on other people's valuations, we will be very vulnerable and prone to feel pain when our "ideality" is questioned. Most people play roles and are afraid to show their real selves because they do not accept their own "nonideality," or they feel embarrassed about who they are. And everybody has their personal "set of shames": to be weak, to ask for help, to cry in public, to be proven wrong when something isn't working out, to make mistakes, to earn little, to have excess weight, to fall in love hopelessly, to be soft, to be sensitive. This is why there are so few people who are truly free, relying not on shame, but rather on their intrinsic worth, which doesn't depend on judgements of others or the quantity of "likes" on social platforms.

Unless you change and become like little children, you will never enter the kingdom of heaven (Matthew 18:3).

Upright position:

- Joy, optimism, love to life, ability to be happy for no reason
- Openness, trust, expression of feelings and needs
- Publicity, success, fulfillment of a dream
- Realization of creative potential (including birth of a child)
- Work with children

Reversed position:

- Inappropriate or destructive behavior model
- Egoism; narcissism; excess demand for love, care, fame, recognition; need for permanent appreciation; lack or excess of confidence
- Loss of taste for life; depression; lack of vitality
- Depreciation of self and one's own needs

JUDGEMENT (20)

(Resurrection)

End of death. Awakening. Mystery of spiritual transformation.

The time has come.

Judgment symbolizes living through a revelation, which becomes the source of change and rebirth. Interaction with this Arcanum is a reopening of oneself on a new level, a radical extension of mind. A paradigm shift, a new way to perceive things, a new meaning, another feeling of life. The Arcanum corresponds to Pluto, and this superior planet transforms things to their core and essence. Their very nature changes.

What you ask about contains the treasure that you seek.

The lesson of this card is to understand that the goal that has been pursued for years really exists. The Arcanum Judgementwakens and lends to realization dormant feelings, ideas, thoughts and revitalizes the forgotten experience that seemed to have become "dead."

Don't try to take with you to a new world somebody or something that doesn't belong there.

Judgement is the call of heaven, the voice that transforms the life of a person who sheds his old shell—antiquated models of life, limiting representations, previous ways of existence, the whole luggage of the previous self—and flies. It is a picture of spiritual rebirth of a person, his redemption and forgiveness. Judgement always symbolizes change of situation, radical changes—where one should go with no fear.

In the life of every person there are moments when it's time to jump into an abyss to finally prove that one was always able to fly.

How does one describe this feeling of freedom? When you hover like a bird in the sky and discover the heights you never knew about. You are still afraid to fall, but with every second the fear wanes.

These wings are truly yours.

Upright position:

- Coming of a new phase in life; shift of paradigm of mindset and values; rediscovering oneself
- Awakening, understanding of the truth

- Redemption of previous mistakes
- Responsible decision, tipping-point situation, important event that requires immediate reaction
- Parting with old decorations (antiquated perception of oneself, way of life, habits, accustomed social circle, etc.)
- Interaction with large social organizations, impact growth, mission

Reversed position:

- Resistance to the New, which has already come (futile, because it can't be avoided); fear to make decision and make a step; confusion
- Crises; payback for actions or lack of ones on the past

The World (21)

End of Journey. Rediscovered paradise. Integrity.
Everything is in its place.

I am the objective of each road.

Eternal renewal of life and cycle, containing the end of everything and returning life to its eternal source. The World personifies serenity of soul, attained after numerous challenges.

Nothing in me is against me.

Total integration of personality, acceptance of all its components, freedom from contradictions. Understanding of one's own inner nature and of surrounding outer forces. Ability to accept the world the way it is, and find one's own place in it. You know who you are. You know why you are.

You are my home.

Living through the Arcanum The World returns basic trust and perception of world changes. But not to the opposite end like "the world is nice and friendly"; rather to "the world is different." Ceases the sensation of competition, struggle for the resource in the sense that those who are "better" and "stronger" will win the most beneficial position, and you'll be left with nothing. With the return of that basic trust leaves the desire to engage in the fight for that resource ... then a feeling appears that everybody has its place, and people do not disturb each other. It is a special feeling to understand that the fight is needless, for the limits are only seeming, and there is a place for everyone (as a chance to realize one's talent and gain recognition).

The wind blows for everyone, not only for the chosen ones. The great sun warms up everybody, and not only the chosen ones. The angels communicate with all of us, and not only to the chosen ones. And the God also communicates with everyone.

God talks to all of us. A person can and is entitled to communicate with God every day on any occasion, just as usual as with friends, children, and relatives. Even more—we already do that every day; this type of messaging is built up in us just like breathing is part of the body. Yes, God is multidimensional—that's why he can communicate to all of us simultaneously, pouring mutually exclusive truths, paradoxes, and tricks. From an earthy human perception, God actually is not paradoxically convex; he is, as mentioned, multidimensional, which is hard to perceive. There are people who audaciously say, "I understand God." Understand and accept are two different things that can be easily entangled. There are people who accept

God, but there is no one who understands God, for he cannot be comprehended by one's mind. Comprehension is logical; it has different dimensionality. Any understanding of God is a simplified projection of his image "from mind." This is probably the source of the paradox, because one can't knit music or cook love in an oven.

I'm here in front of you; I'm everywhere, around you; I'm dwelling in you with a sense of great pleasure. I am the completeness of the being. I am the World, created by God so that he could love you.

Upright position:

- Gaining harmony and peace; satisfaction; resolving contradictions
- Full view of a situation ("to see the whole picture")
- Completion (successful), achievement of a goal, victory, triumph
- Journey, a trip to a foreign place, international relations

Reversed position:

- Frustration; postponed triumph; unfinished work
- Being in the state of appeasement and self-sufficiency became protracted—it is time to start a new cycle; inertia
- Feeling of emptiness after completion of a project ("project" in a broad sense)
- Problems with expansion and the sphere of influence
- Difficulties with setting up trips and journeys

The White Card (–)

Attention of God

I'm looking at you.

The White Card is an Arcanum without a number and a picture. The color white symbolizes concentrated divine energy, before splitting up into a color spectrum. Appearance of The White Card signifies that a person is forming a new personal universe—and the way he is doing it is under the scrutiny of the supreme forces. God is getting close to a person, bringing plenty of energy.

I am concentrated new meaning.

There are special moments in one's life that can be called crucial, so-called tipping points, when one small act can work as a railroad switch. In Tarot they are represented by two Arcana: The White Card and The Fool.

I am a blank page, on which you are writing your history right now.

The future hasn't been formed yet, because it depends on some very important decisions of a person. Even if it's hard to understand logically, the challenge of The White Card is perceived intuitively. Sometimes it feels like fear, anxiety, or "something is happening; I don't understand what it is." Our rational mind is stunned with this divine intervention—as if suddenly the sight is off.

I am the frontier of beginning and consent.

The White Card gives fatality to the message received in the Tarot setup, reinforcing impact of those Arcana around it, whether they are major or minor. Any energy begins to shine more powerfully, as if there has been a special catalyst added to the reaction of its materialization.

To whom much is given—much is expected.

To fulfill the personal super-task translated by The White Card, we receive unlimited opportunities from all the Major Arcana. But such trust from God not only is a gift but carries great responsibility as well. Now it's really important to evaluate the motives of one's own actions and the purity of purpose. The White Card gives no place for a mistake.

UPRIGHT AND REVERSED POSITIONS HAVE THE SAME MEANING:

- Reinforcement of the messages from other cards of the setup (both positive and negative); the most plausible outcome for this situation (detailed information is closed)
- Fatality, inevitability
- Tipping point, event of situation, influencing fate, a new lotus of the future is being formed by the decision of the person, personal responsibility

Minor Arcana
Numerical Cards

ACE OF WANDS

TWO OF WANDS

The Wands

The element of fire in the suit of Wands corresponds to the motivational impulse and intention to act, which are reflected in expression of will, expansion, and resistance to pressures of outer environment. The world is regarded as an object of desire or a rival—from the point of view of the Wands. A distinctive trait of this suit is brightness and expressiveness of demonstration, as well as centering on one's own desires (especially visible in the cards of the court).

THREE OF WANDS

FOUR OF WANDS

Five of Wands

Six of Wands

Seven of Wands

Eight of Wands

Nine of Wands

Ten of Wands

ACE OF WANDS

Will. Dare. Initiative. Social projects aimed to promote own goals. Creative fertilizing force of God.

Ace of Wands is the Arcanum of initiatives, beginnings, and actions. It represents unblocked personal strength and the energy of the yang type, manifested through the "fiery" traits—dynamism, enthusiasm, and fearlessness—a kind of a spiritual erection. Ace of Wands is a potential to get inspired by some business. It is considered that Ace of Wands mainly concerns career questions and social promotion, but it is not always so. Usually a person is quite aware of which part of his life he desires to dare within. Ace of Wands informs that new opportunities are about to come, and so there is sense to prove one's own strengths in the conceived project, show courage, and feel pleasure from it.

Upright position:

- An impulse to create and realize an idea; an initiative, supported by supreme forces
- Social projects aimed to promote one's own goals; actions contributing to elevation of social status and social adaptation
- Initiative, enthusiasm, ambition, passion, energy
- Sexual activity

Reversed position:

- Desire to act in an inappropriate moment; an attempt to leapfrog a step; inefficient actions; an immature project or idea
- Loss of enthusiasm and motivation, lack of confidence, fear of failing; lack of personal energy
- Affairs are delayed, opportunities escape, agreements are canceled

TWO OF WANDS

Between achievements of the past and designs of the future

Two of Wands indicates a new opportunity that the querent is hesitant about: whether to try it or not. A person finds himself on a crossroads and gets stuck, not willing to make a step further in a chosen direction. This threshold can be an affair that a person can't decide whether or not he really wants to get into, or it can be other relations he is unsure about. "A sluggish expression of intent with absence of true willingness to act" (Hajo Banzhaf). After a powerful impulse of Ace, Two of Wands translates as a drawback on motivation and some confusion. A stage of contemplation of one's own abilities; time drags on slowly. One is a process of calm planning, evaluating, considering of strategy, thinking on "what I really want?"

Upright position:

- Contemplation, thinking over, hesitations; lack of interest and motivation; unwillingness to make the next step in a chosen direction
- Neutrality, balance of powers and influences
- Delegation of responsibility

Reversed position:

- Release from a stuck situation; an unexpected turn of events, which will prompt one to act and make decisions

THREE OF WANDS

Start of realization of the conceived and promising prospects

Three of Wands forms a vector of social activity and ability to widely disseminate one's own ideas. Creative energy in a three-pronged flow aims to new goals. Our actions have impact, and we see how the conceived begins to materialize. "Promise" is the keyword for Three of Wands. Under this card, mutual projects are forged, successful cooperation emerges, productive negotiations are made, support is provided, the circle of business partners enriches, business bonds get stronger.

Upright position:
- Enthusiastic planning, interesting prospects
- Successful investment of efforts and resources; ideas get impulse; effective entrepreneurship

Reversed position:
- Slowed-down growth, delay in realization of plans, postponed business
- Futile initiatives
- Incoherent collective actions
- Loss of confidence and enthusiasm, impasse, fear to begin

FOUR OF WANDS

Achievement of first results. Fixation inside the achieved.

The energy of this Arcanum embodies and at the same time limits creative power. What was planned starts to yield results; this creates feelings of stability and security, and anxiety calms. Moreover, it is the Four of Wands that first implies margins and limitations—because it is configured to preserve earned stability and structure. It contains a strong desire to rest after hard work and to enjoy a calm and harmonious (even though boring sometimes) life and its pleasures, which can be bought.

Upright position:

- Remuneration for hard work; visible social achievements (for instance, acquiring one's own place to live)
- Feeling of security and comfort, deserved rest
- Stability, decency, regularity; "life is fixed"

Reversed position:

- Broken stability, disappointing result
- Impasse, stagnation, boredom; prolonged standstill
- Attempt to leave comfort zone
- To act against established traditions

FIVE OF WANDS

Self=affirmation through expansion of personal boundaries and sphere of influence. "Training fight."

The main meaning of Five of Wands is a healthy competition. It contains challenge and tension. The Arcanum offers to try one's own strength, will, skills, talents, and knowledge—in a competition with others. This card talks about fighting for one's own interests among peers "as smart as you." Sometimes Five of Wands resembles a not-so-constructive forum: everybody competes with everybody, and nobody agrees with anybody; still, not everything is real, and it is only a convention. In a worse-case scenario, it is engagement in a fight of ideas, an aggressive discussion environment in which members are negatively induced and do not respect each other; punches are traded, so one has to defend himself anyway he can. In a best-case scenario, it is a useful mind storm that can be used to test one's own ideas through disputes with others.

Upright position:
- Competition, rivalry, contest, challenge, dispute, discussion, argument, some different points of view; the environment resists
- Willingness to prove, to show/express oneself
- Unsatisfied internal tension

Reversed position:
- Passive aggression, hidden conflict
- Unconstructive collective activity; loss of energy
- Dirty fights, crooked competition methods
- Competition is over; discussion exhausted itself

SIX OF WANDS

Social recognition

This Arcanum symbolizes a deserved victory, triumph, and social approval. Your social circle recognizes you as a leader and a winner. Also, it is a compliment to oneself, satisfaction from the performed work. It is what fulfills the integrity of the hero after clashes of the Five of Wands. If we are not ready or are unable to accept our own achievements and value in Six of Wands, then further development will not be successful: there will always be doubts, fears, uncertainty, excuses. Inability to pass the Six of Wands is a perfectionist's curse. The card can't be considered an intimate one—it contains a strong element of pomp, parade, and pathos.

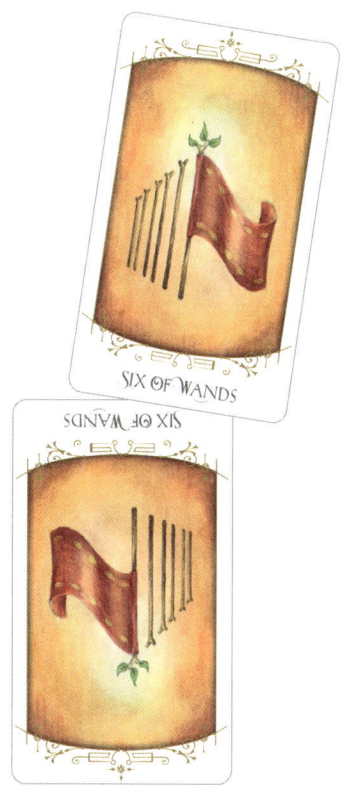

Upright position:

- Success, triumph, deserved victory; appearance of a leader; accepting responsibility and leadership; popularity
- Position, status, achieved through one's own work
- Solution of a problem

Reversed position:

- Loss of a leading position, weakening of authority or influence, unwillingness or inability to accept responsibility
- Loss, defeat
- Dependence on valuation of others; loss of face
- Envy, jealousy

SEVEN OF WANDS

Active defense of one's own frontiers in a real or imaginary conflict

Seven of Wands appears when there are forces on a horizon that appear and intend to confuse us. It encourages us to stand for what we believe in or consider valuable, and prompts us not to compromise or betray our own principles. Sometimes its appearance means that only by making a really desperate step it is possible to win overall in a hopeless struggle or protect our own territory. Seven of Wands gifts stamina, toughness, and courage. Apart from situations of real confrontation, the Arcanum can point at mechanisms of psychological defense (from interventions of the outer world to intrusion of alien attitudes, threatening to ruin habitual internal status quo).

Upright position:

- Protection of a hard-won position, resistance to the external factors; "alone against all"
- Ordeal, challenge
- Confrontation, struggle, courage, decisiveness, fearlessness, dedication

Reversed position:

- Indecisiveness, uncertainty, problems with defending own point of view
- Loss of concentrated energy, "atomization"
- Being paranoid about "everyone's attacking me"

EIGHT OF WANDS
Rapid move forward toward a goal in an environment of benevolent coincidences

Eight of Wands is a favorable Arcanum, pointing at doubtless progress toward a goal. There are lots of air, wind, and aerial flows on this card, and an intense headway. Everything takes shape, and benevolent coincidences emerge. It is essential to pick a direction and move—right now. Eight of Wands is aunique card from the whole deck of 79, clearly indicating that events will occur in the nearest future, earlier than can be believed. It shows that something is changing, that something is in the air and will come before we expect it, and that this process has already started, even if we haven't noticed it yet. There is plenty of libido in Eight of Wands, a lot of excitement—and it especially feels in contrast with a period of stagnation and decadence. It is the Arcanum of self-revelation (letters, messages, talks) in relationships. An unexpected reactivation, clearance of intentions, overcoming of misunderstanding—and even conflict resolution between irreconcilable parties.

Upright position:

- Fast unfolding of events, moving forward, accelerated pace to a goal; short-term success
- New ideas
- Successful circumstances
- Need to take decisions quickly in a changing environment
- Any swift movements (e.g., journeys), information flows (telephone, messenger, emails, etc.)

Reversed position:

- Deceleration of events, slowing down of a process, interferences, obstacles
- Glitch in a process of information exchange (reminds of periods of Mercury in retrograde)
- Incorrect goal-setting
- Lost opportunities

NINE OF WANDS

Defensive position and the power of resistance

The main idea of Nine of Wands is that we have been beaten recently for something or have gotten into a situation that deeply traumatized or frightened us and has left its scars. So now we prefer not to ask for trouble and to stay in a safe shelter, and, at the very least, to recover. Meanwhile, there can be no real threat, but only our recollections of the past troubles. Nine of Wands is an unpleasant and persistent Arcanum; we still protect our interests but do so according to the principle of "keep your guard up and lie low." This self-defense can be interpreted both positively and negatively. This is about obtaining strength to withstand any durability tests—to confront any hardship and reality challenges with dignity (and not desperately quit in front of them). This is the card of will and internal strength of a querent. In its negative aspect, Nine of Wands means that a person is not free from his past and hence does not trust his future.

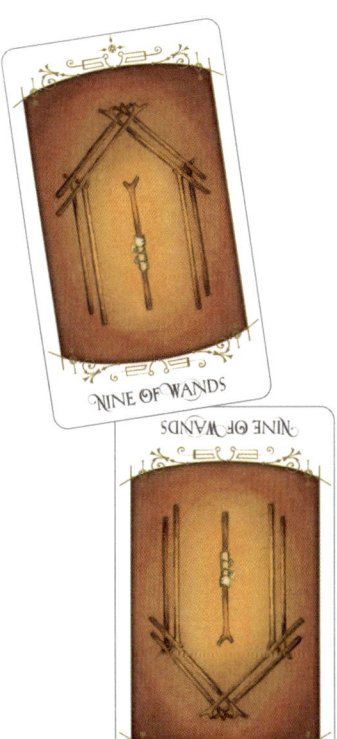

Upright position:

- Wariness, tension, anticipation of a threat; reliving past traumatic experience; mistrust
- Reluctance to change, conservatism
- Patience, resilience, self-possession, discipline, caution
- A period of recovery; parsimonious energy expense

Reversed position:

- Exaggeration of possibilities, overestimation of powers, loss of vigilance; exhaustion, nervous breakdown, extreme fatigue
- Deactivation of protective mechanisms, coming out of shell; attempting to overcome one's fear and gain new experiences; attempting to establish contact
- Turning inward, total isolation

TEN OF WANDS

Burden of social masks multiplied by ambitions, fears, and a false sense of duty

Total responsibility and a will to take over more and more (what for?) led to the point where the burden of responsibilities became overwhelmingly heavy. Ten of Wands is the Arcanum of tension, overload, and burning out. An unpleasant state where tasks and things begin to drop out of mind and hands, and an impulse to blow this cart all away and leave for nowhere begins to mount. At its core this burden is only complexes and fears—the fear to be disliked, to be unable to please, to turn out to be a bad person (wife, husband, worker, son, daughter . . .) in somebody's eyes. This, plus arrogance ("I can do anything"), forces one to take over too much. Ten of Wands marks the final stage of the fiery period of assertion of one's own material-social "self," and a person turns into his inner world, transitioning to the period of the development of soul—comprehension of the sensual sphere (which starts under the Ace of Cups).

The lesson of Ten of Wands is not difficult: the difference between coercion and endeavor is that in the first case we ignore our resources and limitations, and in the second one we leverage them.

Upright position:

- Overload, fatigue, burning out; too many things to do at the same time; backbreaking circumstances; excessive ambitions
- Hyperresponsibility, hypercontrol, perfectionism, workaholism; intention to do everything by oneself
- Sense of duty, "salvationism"

Reversed position:

- Devolving of responsibility; delegation; arrival of an assistant
- Crush of ambitions; nervous meltdown; "a man has broken"

The Cups

The suit of Cups is connected to the sphere of feelings, emotions, empathic experience, and emotional inspiration; it represents the element of water. It symbolizes our sensual experiences—both superficial and deep, short lived and relatively constant, pleasurable and unpleasant. It is believed that this suit is connected to intuition, but this can be agreed on only in part. The intuition of Cups is specifically emotional experience, ownership to something or somebody; a substance very mutable and fluid, not distinguishing between self and "something else." The whole Cups experience is connected to erosion of personal boundaries and perception of another (person or event) as part of oneself and oneself as its part. Hence, associations of the suit with the spectrum of love relationships, with creative experience (as a merge with some aesthetic ideal), and also with psychological dependencies (on a person, a state, a drug, etc.).

Five of Cups

Six of Cups

Seven of Cups

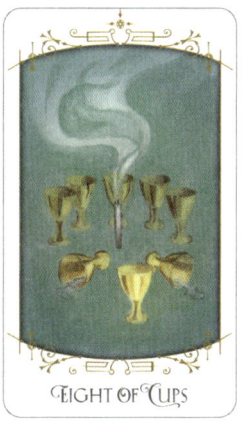
Eight of Cups

Nine of Cups

Ten of Cups

ACE OF CUPS
The source of happiness

Aces in Tarot are the root of a suit, the concentrator of its potential, its "semen." Every Ace symbolizes opportunity of the most bright and precise expression of the quality of a suit, as if you hold a powerful battery charged with a certain energy. Because the suit of Cups reflects the sphere of human emotions, its Ace represents the source of emotional impression. This Arcanum can be named one of the most pleasant in the entire deck. Getting close to the energy of the Ace of Cups provides new opportunities on the emotional level, filling us up from the inside—with joy, delight, feelings of happiness. Ace of Cups often reflects the beginning of a new relationship, a new love affair, which has all the chances to grow into a really deep love. It can also be fascination with a new idea, a new project, music, any action or event that forms a bright emotional impact, "fresh emotional afterglow," real internal art. The Cup itself is an archetypical symbol of femininity, the sacred woman's womb producing the flow of eternal life and eternal love, the Holy Grail. In the same way, the Ace of Cups is an inexhaustible source of our soul, which contains in itself the great potential of love—from sensuality to the mystical pursuit of Absolute. This feeling is like a path that leads us to the greatest spiritual level.

Upright position:
- Feeling of happiness, internal fulfillment, trust; source of joy
- Spiritual disclosure; readiness to accept and forgive; mercy
- Emotional uplift, falling in love; a chance for a great Love
- Inspiration, creativity

Reversed position:
- Emotional emptiness, "hunger," depression
- "Feelings dried up"; disappointment, grudge, nuisance, self-pity
- Emotional exhaustion
- Purposeless waste of creative powers
- Unrequited or spurned love; missed chance for a big Love

TWO OF CUPS

Intimacy of the two. Reciprocal feelings.

Two of Cups often means emotional unity, perception of the other as one's own twin, reflection, "same as me." It resembles an encounter with oneself but in another body. Usually it's a pleasant start of a contact, the stage of intense love feelings, followed by diffusion of personal borders, and, in the case of a stable relationship, a kind of an established form where the two participants play the roles of interconnected communicating vessels. On the symbolic plane, Two of Cups represents an "alchemic marriage"—all kinds of unions, including intellectual and creative, situations of cooperation and cocreation. Also, Two of Cups points at the harmonic exchange between yin and yang parts of the soul (possibly inside a single person, which means self-acceptance, establishing relations with oneself). On a deeper level, the Arcanum describes that fundamental factor that how the others treat us reflects our own treatment of self.

Upright position:

- Connection, encounter, contact, force of attraction; reciprocal love feelings; energy interexchange; respect and cooperation
- Mutual understanding, emotional intimacy, empathy; ability to share one's own feelings (even pain) with another and to accept another person's feelings; forgiveness and reconciliation
- Equal relationship, partnership
- Rejoining a lost (disintegrated) part of oneself

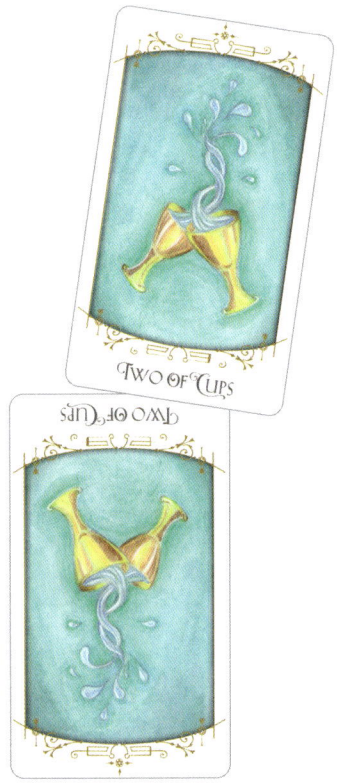

Reversed position:

- Loss of intimacy and empathetic contact; inability to understand each other; incompatibility, irritation; quarrel, conflict
- Separation, disintegration, a meeting that didn't take place
- Disrupted trust, disappointment
- Unrequited love feeling

THREE OF CUPS

A celebration for the three. Drunkenness with joys of life.

Three of Cups points at the creation of a pleasant emotional field that is less intimate than with Two of Cups, framed more socially, and suggests free communication among several subjects. Usually it is a pleasant company of friends, but, as with any Three, it can be attributed to a love triangle—but in this case it either satisfies everybody or the borders between its participants are undefined, and it's unclear who in fact is who to whom. On Three of Cups we perceive the space as a source of abundancies and joy and are willing to share this emotional grace with others. The important thing is that this celebration of soul wouldn't turn into a wild bacchanalia with a heavy morning hangover.

Upright position:

- Getting joys, enjoying life, optimism; "drunkenness," exaltation
- Party, celebration, merry collective; friendship, joviality, openness, expansion of relationships, increase in social contacts
- Unions and alliances; support from peers; recognition, popularity
- Generosity, abundance
- Love triangles

Reversed position:

- Cloying; abuse of joy led to exhaustion of perception
- "Blue Monday" (party is over; time to work)
- Disappointment; desired joys passed by
- Problems with unions and alliances; expulsion from a circle or a community
- Dependencies, addictive behavior

FOUR OF CUPS

Emotional stagnation

The celebration of Three of Cups can't last forever. Its side effect is cloying, which is reflected by Four of Cups. This Arcanum resembles stale waters, where our soul got immersed. Receptors of emotional perception are depleted, consciousness gets stuck in repeating experiences, and the same words sound in the head with the same emotional subtext. A person rejects new opportunities and is reluctant to develop creative talents, to begin new projects, to meet new people—he thinks that all of that is not interesting and is senseless. Four of Cups is a card of the first existential disappointment in earthly life and its joys. After first successes in that endeavor, first joys and achievements, comes the feeling that "not all of this is what it should be." In fact, Four of Cups informs that it's time to aim for the values of a finer and more elevated nature, to feel the life as an inexhaustible source of opportunities, hidden in itself, and to evoke creative vitality.

Upright position:

- Apathy, moping, cloying, gloom, boredom, feeling of grudge and nuisance; absence of interest and motivation; nothing brings joy; fixation on the same experiences; fruitless reflection
- Unjustified expectations, internal dissatisfaction with self and others
- Stability, stagnation, impasse, routine; unwillingness to take risks

Reversed position:

- Seeking new opportunities; a chance to come out of boredom and stop expecting salvation from the outside
- Something new enters life; it brings revival of feelings

FIVE OF CUPS

Emotional crises. Crying over.

Five of Cups resembles the state of separation from the source of life, which brings confusion and grieving, as if something important was lost. This card is connected to strong emotions (and this is how it differs from apathetic Four of Cups); it can be the strong disappointment of a heartache, but more often it's a mental pain that can't be overcome early on, and emotional crises and depression could also be indicated. Something that carried great expectations with it is left behind, and this pain shall be well thought out and lived through. The trap of Five of Cups is getting stuck in sorrow. Those who looks only behind won't notice love, even if it's quite close. This is such a deep immersion into the thought of one's own loss that a person ceases paying attention to other opportunities; still, we live in a bivalent world where every negative event is equaled by a positive one and where almost any loss can be looked at as a gain. Even if we missed some opportunities and lost what was valuable to us, we would have to turn the page and move on.

Upright position:
- Sorrow, emptiness, weakness, depression, self-pity; "want to cry"
- State of abandonment, discard, rejection
- Loss, breakup, separation; frustrations, regrets of the missed opportunities, regret about the past

Reversed position:
- Recovery after loss and emotional crises; crying over is over; we find sources that can feed our present and our future
- Recovery of old bonds; intention to return into relationships

SIX OF CUPS

Somebody or something good from the past

Having survived the crises of the Five, Six of Cups reflects the ability to find resources for recovery in the past. We return to a harmonious state with the images of our own subconscious, addressing something good from the past, experiencing regress of emotional perception of the world, as if we are children once again. Six of Cups is the Arcanum of nostalgia; with it come the memories of the past passions, people return, and lost objects are found. What seemed lost is returned in the Sixes. Presence of this card tells about awakening of forgotten wishes, past aspirations, intentions, and plans. Something clearly remembers the past—people, places, events . . . Under this card the pages of one's own book of life are flipped through. Sometimes Six of Cups is named "what has vanished," but the thing is, it hasn't vanished at all. It can't vanish. Under Six of Cups, better times are not coming—better times are *returning*. Returning the inner belief that there is happiness, that it can happen in principle, and that if you were happy once, then you can remember how it feels and regain this feeling.

Upright position:

- Pleasant memories of the past, looking back; returning of ideas and projects from the past; reliance on the past experience
- Meeting of old friends, coming of old acquaintances; support from a person from the past
- Return to home country, return to childhood
- Comfortable and safe emotional state; trust; reconciliation; to share feelings

Reversed position:

- Parting with the past, overcoming childish ideals and dreams, coming of age, leaving of "parents' nest"; aiming for the future (sometimes followed by ignoring past experiences)
- Painful nostalgia for the past (relations, work, etc.); inability to live in the present; inadequate evaluation of a situation
- Improper infantilism

SEVEN OF CUPS

Rich imagination. Fascination. Lack of critical attitude.

Seven of Cups represents feelings of sickly unsatisfied demands in something related to emotional, creative, or spiritual spheres, and the conflict between the desired and the real. Every Seven in Tarot offers opportunity for personal growth, but every time it is also accompanied with its own risk. Seven of Cups brings trials of illusions that are created by the psyche. In their core they are temptations. The mind is overwhelmed with multiple subconscious images; they lure and promise to fulfill one's wishes. It could be that these tenuous phantoms are in fact reflections of different opportunities, but their quantity throws you off; they are too fantastic to be true. In the energy of Seven of Cups, a person struggles to understand what he really wants. As a rule, this card comes as a precursor to sobering, which means . . . disappointment. On the other side, it is a kind of visualization—a person draws in his mind different variants of events, all that could be. Visualizing success sometimes is important.

Upright position:

- Illusions, unfounded fantasies; drift from reality; to confuse wishful thinking, "to build castles in the sky"; temptations, seductions, drunkenness with perspectives
- Inclination to deceit and self-deception; altered states of conscious
- Difficulties of choice, inability to make decisions and define; "dreaming" instead of "acting"
- Imagination as a resource; work with images; creativity, artful thinking

Reversed position:

- Awakening, enlightenment, parting with illusions; understanding of false expectations
- To define the intention and focus on it
- Lack of imagination and fantasy

EIGHT OF CUPS

Ability to say "goodbye" and let go

Under Eight of Cups, one's own state, way of life, or usual decorations (for instance, relations or work) look spent and worn out like cloths. This Arcanum tells of a change in paradigm in perception of reality—a person realizes the impossibility of the way he used to live and, by his own will, leaves something familiar for the unknown. Eight of Cups is a harbinger of changes in life, which at the end can turn out to be as positively perceived as they are negatively and heavily perceived now. A person is involved in the process of parting with the past; a transitional period comes, a "great exodus," when his life goals and priorities change. The specificity of Eight of Cups is that such a decision is willful but is taken with a heavy heart in a situation that is felt to be hopeless; to say it more precisely: there is only one way out—to leave. In contrast to Five of Cups, nothing is toppled or spilled here; it's just that the time has come to move on. And there is plenty of decisiveness—a person is guided by a certain force, and as bad as he may feel, the call of the way and the internal encouragement will not leave him alone, providing necessary energy.

Upright position:

- Willful leaving of a stagnant situation; acceptance of inability to fix it
- Parting ways, breakup, rejection, renunciation; "easier to leave than to stay"; heavy farewell
- Disappointment, sorrow, longing; loss of energy, loss of interest, tiredness; depression
- Reassessing of self and the reality; beginning of spiritual search

Reversed position:

- Inertia, immobility, incompleteness; stagnation
- Fear to leave or let go what is obsolete
- Feeling of despair

NINE OF CUPS
"Loaded up"

Nine of Cups is the Arcanum of dreams come true and at the same time of an emotional saturation, even overload. Nine cups become a wall, protecting the satisfied Ego from adversity. In this sense, Nine of Cups exhibits escapism—to live in one's own reality. "All that I wanted, I got it. What else can be desired—I don't know." This Arcanum describes an emotional reward that we get when we are satisfied with what's happening and with ourselves. The decision to destroy the integrity of this state or not is assigned to ourselves. Nevertheless, it's uneasy to destroy the space of Nine of Cups. It literally feeds us with happiness, coming from the very depths of a peaceful soul, and in this sense provides a special (and meaningful!) spiritual experience. The main thing is not to forget to share this energy with others—"from the excess."

Upright position:
- Satisfaction, well-being, saturation of sensual hunger, joy of life
- Feeling of security and fulfillment of desires; relaxation; absence of anxiety
- Celebration, party; a chance to indulge oneself
- A talent to create something "tasty," in demand

Reversed position:
- Overload, dissatisfaction (pleasures don't bring joy anymore); overindulgence
- Egocentricity, complacency, greed
- Immoderation (gluttony, alcoholism, etc.)
- Loss of the feeling of stability, security, balance

TEN OF CUPS

Feel happy and generously share this with whom you love.

TThis is a state where a person begins to understand the immaculacy of love, the things he needs to be happy, and a feeling of deep gratitude for the chance to meet those very special people. With this card comes a feeling of satisfaction into life from relationships, both romantic and friendly, saying that the emotional potential of a person has developed to its peak; he feels a divine blessing. It is the Arcanum of cohesion and convergence, when one miraculously loses "individual self" and becomes an integral part of the loved ones and those who love back. The feelings are open for the world and are presented without fear of being unaccepted, misunderstood, or rejected. But the grace of Ten of Cups hides the barely subtle (but nevertheless distinct) idea that this idyll is not the end of the Way, for as precious as it can be, the call of the spirit demands one to move on, toward new ideas (Ace of Swords).

Upright position:

- Feelings of divine blessing and integrity; deep spiritual satisfaction
- Emotional exaltation; peace, harmony, trust, convergence, acceptance, mutual understanding
- Happiness among other people (family, friends, colleagues, et al.); willingness to share love with others
- Completeness, perfection, satisfaction

Reversed position:

- Emotional dissatisfaction; lost internal integrity; devastation and overload
- Loss of the feeling of emotional intimacy (in a family, a collective, etc.); quarrels and conflicts
- Rupture of family bonds; leaving homeland; "the nest is empty"; negation of family values

ACE OF SWORDS

TWO OF SWORDS

The Swords

The suit of Swords represents cognitive, mental, and educational spheres of human experience. It is the clear understanding of how something and generally everything is set up and works—still, irrespective of how it is really set up. With this suit we connect the function of learning how the world goes and consciousness and comprehension of self and one's own actions, as well as the idea of rules according to which has been created and functions as a "mini-universe" of each person. These are logical explanations of things, human behavior and all causal relationships—perceived from the outside.

THREE OF SWORDS

FOUR OF SWORDS

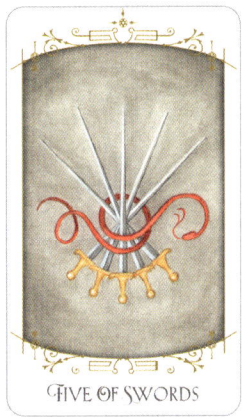
FIVE OF SWORDS

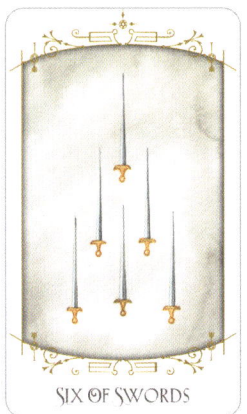
SIX OF SWORDS

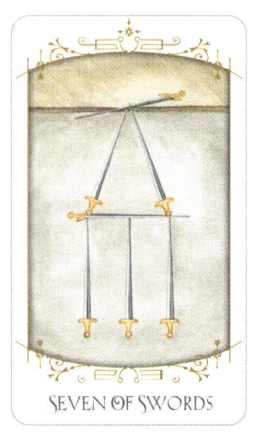
SEVEN OF SWORDS

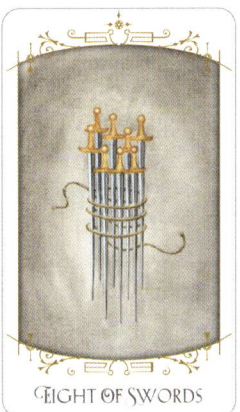
EIGHT OF SWORDS

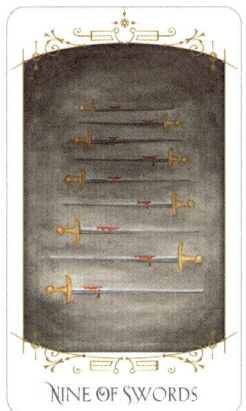
NINE OF SWORDS

TEN OF SWORDS

ACE OF SWORDS

The spirit of the truth. A rational idea. The final argument. Uncompromising solution.

The Ace of Swords is an exceptional and clear understanding, a revelation, a clear vision of the meaning of what's happening. The appearance of a new idea expanding consciousness reminds one of a "mental initiation," like a connection to something new. This Ace indeed is a gift of mind—as the ability of mind to cut off the unnecessary, to divide, and to get to the very core in the most clear and liberating form. This is a situation when a person has cleared up a lot for himself and gotten to know what he wants to do further—sharply separating what he wants from what he doesn't. One of the meanings of the Arcanum is a limit, a frontier, an edge. We can talk about setting up borders or drawing a line under something. Ace of Swords can be a tough decision, taken from the perspective of power, will, and reason, against all sentiments. Anyway, with this Ace comes crystal clearance in something, whether it is a solution to a hard problem, a confrontation with a partner, or overcoming doubts. It is a card of inner truth, strictness, and firm principles.

Upright position:

- Clearing up, figuring out, constructing objective picture (for instance, an explanatory talk); "to set the record straight"
- A rational exciting idea, a declaration of a point of view, a final argument; a strong-willed decision
- Assurance, clarity, fearlessness; honesty

Reversed position:

- Weakness of will and mind; inability to formulate an intention; apathy
- Uncontrolled destructive power
- Obsession with an idea ended up in havoc; a crisis
- Depression, suicidal thoughts, autoaggression
- Conception, pregnancy

TWO OF SWORDS
Dilemma.

If Ace of Swords is the power or clarity, then Two of Swords is the power of doubts. While Ace of Swords denotes one single idea, Two of Swords contains two opposite points of view, trying to establish a balanced truce. Crossed swords symbolize the boundaries of intellect preventing access to intuitive knowledge. There are niggling reflections on Two of Swords; it looks like a temporary dead end or a process of thinking over: What shall I do? How do I "marry" those contradictions? The situation is ambivalent, perspectives are unclear, internal tension remains—the choice is yet to be made.

Upright position:
- Hesitations, doubts, reflections; protracting attempts to find a rational compromise; postponing making a decision; attempts to "figure out"; waiting
- Outside truce; hidden conflict of two powers
- Unwillingness to see the truth; denial
- Indecisiveness, contradictions; withdrawal

Reversed position:
- Things moved on after external impact
- Forced decision unsupported internally, followed by strong anxiety

THREE OF SWORDS

Ideals are put to the test.

Three of Swords is a choice made in defiance of feelings; a person has to reject or renege something that has value for him. The Arcanum symbolizes the consequences of aiming for the unreachable ideal paired to ignoring reality. It dissects the haze of emotional idealization, brings some kind of collision with what it's about in reality, and this "truth of life" provokes painful feelings. Three of Swords requires producing the final answer, which is hard to do but necessary. It is a kind of initiation, a dedication through a painful challenge and a breakup with the previous life.

Upright position:

- Deconstruction of illusions, a conflict of mind and heart, a bitter truth; a hard choice in favor of arguments of the mind; a painful experience
- A breakup, separation
- Onerous emotional state (disappointment, living through losses, credibility crisis, pity for oneself, unrequited love; state after traumatic events)

Reversed position:

- Recovery after traumatic events; overcoming crisis
- Continuing grief, sorrow uncried

FOUR OF SWORDS

Sanctuary where transformation takes place.
Meditation for recovery.

Four of Swords is the Arcanum of interrupted activity and forced calm. For many it is not a pleasure; less often this card is enjoyed as an opportunity to let go, get away, collect one's thoughts, be around oneself, and take a breath. But this time-out is highly necessary now. It bestows a sanctuary from fuss, even if a person himself painfully regards it as exile; it is what is called a retreat. It is a tomb and a cradle at the same time, a place of accumulation, concentration, and transformation; in this sealed environment, like in an airtight retort of an alchemist, a transformational process shall happen.

Upright position:
- Forced calm, temporary relief, accumulation of powers; isolation, absence
- Deep concentration, meditation; internal concentration, analysis, self-discovery; spiritual practice, retreat
- Conscious process of acceptance ("containment") of different point of view
- Truce, lull

Reversed position:
- End of period of isolation or rest, resumption of contacts with the outer world
- Awakening, readiness to act; return to work

FIVE OF SWORDS

Provocation of the worst qualities

Five of Swords represents a period of aggressive, destructive thinking, when embittered Ego craves only one thing—revenge at all costs. Adequate perception of what's going on is impossible—a negative mental program distorts the picture and requires immediate reaction: "Ah, so! Take that!"). Five of Swords can mean escalation of a conflict, a vile act, a low blow, treachery, meanness, some kind of intrigue, and/or hidden or apparent hostility. Nonetheless, the card doesn't point to whether all these malicious acts come from us or we find ourselves to be involved in this nefarious story as a victim. But even "victory" in the case of Five of Swords will not long please the winner. There is a lot of poison—and it will hurt not only the defeated one.

Upright position:
- Conflict; open aggression or passive-aggressive behavior, appetite for revenge, "to act out of spite," dirty gesture, villainy, betrayal; shuttered trust
- Competitive struggle with the help of dirty and treacherous acts, to get what is desired by any means
- Destructive thinking (including toward oneself); self-incrimination, self-abasement; irrational fear, panic attack

Reversed position:
- A devastating defeat
- Consequences of vile thoughts and deeds

SIX OF SWORDS

Cognition. "New horizons." Expansion of personal mental universe.

On Five of Swords we faced destructive consequences of this episode of a personal story. On the basis of the principle of the suit, Six of Swords helps to restore and rewire the ripped picture of the world: pairing of reason and consequence, analysis of what has happened. This is restoration of intellectual power willing to integrate past shocks into a new explanation. The appropriate phrase for Six of Swords is "way out" (of a difficult, messed-up, joyless situation) by implementing a new vision and changing paradigm. These are new life perspectives, new goals, and new means. We have to head toward new life shores. What this journey will bring is unclear. But what could be more appealing to the freedom-loving and curious Swords than the state of exploring, moving from the known, but unsatisfying to the total uncertainty?

Upright position:

- Step out to an unexplored territory in a broad sense: examination of an unknown object; obtaining new experience
- Expansion of intellectual vision of a situation; new look; change of internal reference points
- Events related to intellectual development (acquisition and analysis of new information, training)
- Physical movements and mobility of any kind (journey, trip, relocation, etc.)

Reversed position:

- Unwillingness to move (both in direct and indirect sense); resistance to new perspectives, rejection of new beginnings
- Feeling of a dead end and the impossibility of finding a solution
- Delays and setbacks

SEVEN OF SWORDS

Test of intellectual skills connected to cunning and adventurism. Trickery and diplomacy dangerously close to scam and lies.

Seven of Swords describes an attempt to find a solution to a complicated situation, to avoid conflict, and to get what is desired with the help of some tricks and schemes. It points at the necessity to be smart, to think several steps ahead, and to employ strategic "subterfuges." It may not be the best kind of behavior, but sometimes we need to act that way—and we already understood it when we were children ("You can't tell all the truth to your parents, can you?"). The question is how big a lie is it, what is it about, and what kind of consequences may be brought? Seven of Swords is crooked; it raises the question of plausibility of intentions and ethics of actions. At the same time this Arcanum can just inform that there will be a test on how effective your mind is, and that you will have to seek solutions to an uneasy situation.

Upright position:
- Ingenuity, inventiveness, resourcefulness, deviousness, gumption; flexibility
- Calculation of options, preparing for a "long con"
- Dishonesty, treachery, manipulations, intrigues, "sleazy" situation
- Escaping from responsibility ("getting away with it"); attempts to avoid direct talk; stockpiling of distracting explanations

Reversed position
- "A long con" has failed with a bang; discovery of a lie or betrayal, exposure
- Lack of ingenuity to calculate the consequences
- Unwillingness to engage in a dubious scam
- Bringing back of the stolen (in literal and figurative meaning)

EIGHT OF SWORDS

Imaginary limits becoming socially visible

Eight of Swords is the card of limitations. It describes the states of restrain, helplessness, limitation—all those situations where a person doesn't feel free and can't act according to his or her own desires. Eight of Swords is filled with self-paralysis and confinement. All attempts to act differently come upon resistance. Eight of Swords shows that we ourselves repress some part of our personality. Often it is inner barriers or bans where we usually employ ourselves, but still try to find some outer reason. Its common example is a typical "yes, but . . .". Eight of Swords illustrates the power of outsider judgements and critics strengthening confusion and uncertainty in the accuracy of one's own acts. In the energy of this Arcanum, a personality fails to develop because of a fear to act "inadequately" (from the social point of view) or it is an unwillingness to pay the consequences. A person allowed somebody else to administer everything in his life. He gave away power, gave away strength, became a hostage of what does or doesn't somebody else do, and stopped expecting anything from himself as if nothing depends on him.
Why? What makes him act so?

Upright position:

- Absence of freedom, self-restrictions, uncertainty, unfounded fears; narrow and constrained views; subjective internal barriers, inner bans (often unconscious)
- Fear to occupy a certain position, to protect oneself; fear to take a decision
- Limitation of rights and opportunities; facing of critics or censorship

---

Reversed position:

- Overcoming of tight situations, blocks, and psychological barriers
- Reevaluation of situation and own abilities; progress

NINE OF SWORDS

Destructive self=analysis, self=blaming and self= punishment

Nine of Swords is described as an unmanageable wave of anxiety, longing, fear, guilt, and terror in the face of a life, which uplifts in the subconscious. It denotes a person's consciousness immersed into the darkness, into the subconscious possession, rejecting rational exhortations. Compulsive thoughts have us as if under siege. All that comes from inside, though; we are sure the threat is directed from the outside. Nine of Swords tells us that there's something inducing strong, unbearable anxiety—literally immersing us into a personal hell of our own negative thoughts. In the worst-case scenario, the Arcanum indicates a trial by losses (or a fear of loss) and pain. It is a state when it seems that the whole world is against you, and God has left you. One can't wish away the nightmare of Nine of Swords—this suffering has to be lived through: literally by coming through this experience, the source of fear will be found and realized on the deeper level.

Upright position:
- "A soul is mauled"; despair, remorse, feeling of guilt, self-loathing, resignation; feeling of God absence
- Escalation of longing; fears, bad expectations, thought of expected problems; anticipation of a breakup
- Inadequate evaluation of the real situation (often with exaggeration of a danger and infusion of negative thoughts)

Reversed position:
- Acceptance of a situation, beginning of recovery
- End of self-torment, forgiving oneself

TEN OF SWORDS

"Don't be afraid of death. While you are alive it is still not here, and when you are dead—it's already not here."

Ten of Swords is a merciless Arcanum. The bad side of it is that everything is bad, and the good side is that it won't get any worse. And only after having reached the bottom can we kick off from it and emerge on the surface as if we have just been born again. Like the Arcanum of Death, Ten of Swords personifies the finish, the end of some difficult and dark period, an end of something—decay, demarcation. Ten of Swords demands "Enough!" and advises you to let go of something precious—being the necessary condition of liberation. Demolition of past notions (of a certain area of life or a certain issue), crying away and accepting an irreversible loss, slowly collecting what can be useful one day, what can be leveraged in a new cycle—all these are the experiences of Ten of Swords. Having passed through the challenges of Nine of Swords, a person decides to put his sufferings to an end—and to meet his nightmare face to face. To accept it. And by doing this, he persuades the fate that he deserves a better fortune, though by the look he can seem pitiful and tortured. But the destiny knows to admire the inner rebellion.

And its gift to a hero is a dawn of a new day and a new life.

Upright position:

- Plans are in ruins, fight is lost; "the bottom"
- Finish, end, period; loss of illusions, acceptance of the inevitable, giving up struggle
- Distant perception of one's own suffering
- Exhaustion, depletion, drain; "resetting to zero," purge, release
- End of cycle; painful transition to a new life
- Trust to the fate

Reversed position:

- Beginning of a new cycle; hope; renascence
- Change in perception of a situation, awareness of the accuracy of what is happening

ACE OF PENTACLES

TWO OF PENTACLES

The Pentacles

The suit of Pentacles is related to production, recycling, and investment of material and physical resources. It covers labor questions (process organization, interactions), all monetary and asset questions, all "possessions" and physical aspects (condition and needs of the body, starting from nutrition and sleep and to the need in one's own safe place; physical condition). The paradox of Pentacles is that the "product" of this suit is created slowly but in case of improper handling can be "spoiled" and "spent" quite quickly.

THREE OF PENTACLES

FOUR OF PENTACLES

FIVE OF PENTACLES

SIX OF PENTACLES

SEVEN OF PENTACLES

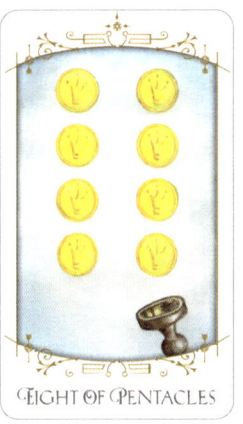
EIGHT OF PENTACLES

NINE OF PENTACLES

TEN OF PENTACLES

ACE OF PENTACLES
A gift from Fortune

Ace of Pentacles is libido being materially impersonated. The golden disc radiates with material well-being and feels like a gift from Fortune. Income, abundance of resources, and, first of all, earthly. It is one of the luckiest (in common sense) cards. It talks about the opportunity to find something constant and significant, to put basis for something robust, continuous, and valuable. The spectrum is wide—from financial success to spiritual enrichment. Ace of Pentacles says that well-being is a totally natural state of a man. It does not oppose but, rather, assists in revealing one's own spirituality and creative potential in this world. If we lack something, then there may not be enough "us" for something to contain it within? We are so used to always being hungry that it becomes our second self. And abundancy is always here, always near.

Upright position:
- Favorable conditions to gain some material goods (a good purchase, a precious gift, financial profit, increase in salary, bonus, reward, profitable investment, access to resources)
- Stability, security, comfort; great physical compatibility with a partner; physical health
- "Gift"; something weighty, fulfilling and really precious that chases away sentiments of deficit and hunger

---

Reversed position:
- Absorption in questions of stability, security, and financial guarantees; riches that don't bring happiness; greed, "hunger"
- Unsustainably and unwisely spent resource; Delays, postponements, and other problems with financial flows

TWO OF PENTACLES
Art of being flexible

Two of Pentacles is the Arcanum of adaptation and maneuverability (sometimes an excessive one). It resembles an attempt to control several things, situations, projects, and relations at the same time. For a modern person this is quite normal, something similar to a usual day-to-day stress of multitasking and unstoppable tuning. Two of Pentacles is a dynamic balance. Unstable, sometimes this Two makes you nervous, sometimes giving too much fuss, but it is still there. One of the keywords for Two of Pentacles is "cycle." Its wisdom is that ups are followed by downs and vice versa, and this is natural. According to Two of Pentacles, a person is capable of adjusting to almost any circumstances, and there are always opportunities in our lives for development and rebalance of situations. Their quantity is limited only by one thing—flexibility of our minds to employ some irony toward what is happening.

Upright position:
- Controlled changes, to "juggle" circumstances
- Adaptation, ability to adapt in a changing environment; inclination for situational compromises
- Ambiguity, volatility
- Doing several things at a time; fuss
- Correspondence, negotiations, settlements

Reversed position:
- Mess; delay; distortion of loss of information (for example, mistakes or falsification of documents, bureaucratic protractions, rumors, loss of messages and letters, tardiness)
- Fail to fulfill promises and commitments; inefficient actions; volatility

THREE OF PENTACLES
Power of practical creation

Three of Pentacles symbolizes materialization of energy and the physical embodiment of the Divine plan. Work with physical materials—explicitly or subconsciously—as a magical ritual. Transformation of matter unifies a man with God through an act of creation. Three of Pentacles describes a mighty trinity of the body, the mind, and the soul, constructing visible structures in the three-dimensional space. It is a card of specific deeds, work, stabilization of the achieved, and putting things in order, as well as practical learning, professional formation, skills upgrade, and development of new competencies. Three of Pentacles does not promise a mind-blowing result but supports sustainable progress in realization of ideas. Having the Three of Pentacles in readings indicates the importance of unifying efforts and exchanging ideas in any, even the most individual, task. So, get to work!

Upright position:
- Development of skills and mastery, professionalism; constructive creative activities; integrity
- Cooperation, efficient teamwork; reciprocal help, mutual understanding
- Improvement of an existing system in terms of labor organization or processes
- Readiness to receive constructive feedback
- Acquisition of a diploma, qualification; professional growth

Reversed position:
- Insufficient qualification, incompetency
- Low quality of work, "botch," negligence, inaccuracy
- Failed interview; loss of work; dismissal
- Workaholism; behind the excessive attention to details, the whole picture and the sense are lost

FOUR OF PENTACLES

"I won't let anyone take what's mine!"

On Four of Pentacles the suit stabilizes for the first time—it almost freezes. Achievement of a certain economic stability followed by a feeling of security puts us at risk of degradation of mind, locked in a perimeter of absolutization of material guarantees, negating any further development out of fear of losing what has been "earned with sweat and blood." We are ready to abandon communication with others or accompany it with endless calculations of "who owes what to whom." The card describes something hard-earned but with a certain safety margin. It can be anything—business, health, relations, or a system of values. This "something" looks robust but in fact lacks adaptive abilities and the life itself. All energy here is spent to conserve status quo, which becomes an obsessive idea. Nothing goes, but nothing can come as well. The best that this card can give is self-discipline, practical approach, ability to rely only on oneself, and the skill to cope with a difficult life situation by keeping control and composure. At the same time, Four of Pentacles is the card of egoism, fear, control, and excessive caution. Keywords of Four of Pentacles are "to have," "to possess," or "to conserve." It doesn't like "to risk," "to give," or "to open up."

Upright position:

- Control and protection of resources, accumulation of material assets, frugality, economy
- Stability, conservatism; fear of change, fear of loss, preoccupation with future
- Greed, egoism, suspicion
- Keeping borders; protection, armor

Reversed position:

- Loss of material stability, financial losses; inability to keep possessions and protect savings; squandering
- Decrease of material preoccupation; readiness to share part of resources; liberation from an affection that restricted
- Decrease of control, release

FIVE OF PENTACLES

Is it possible to keep spiritual and complete when feeling sick and out of sorts?

Five of Pentacles represents the period of inner degradation, when we feel miserable and left behind as well as unsatisfied, and sometimes literally finding ourselves in restrained conditions. But more often this anxiety is not produced by external problems. Such feelings come because of loss of imaginary security, which yesterday (on the previous Arcanum) was our stronghold. The true self, striving for development, was repressed and now a will to change forcefully punches this state, producing painful crises. The Arcanum reflects deficiency—of physical strengths, material resources, self-confidence, or simple human warmth. At the same time, Five of Pentacles indicates the need to keep humble and maintain a spiritual position under any circumstances. It reminds us that such challenges are transitory.

Upright position:

- Going out of a comfort zone; anxiety and disquiet; fear of losses and deprivations
- Financial crises, material instability; expenses out of control
- Feeling one's own lameness, abandonment, and being in need; "deficiency thinking," complaints
- Opportunity of spiritual growth via humbleness and acceptance of hollowness of physical possessions; transformation of Ego ("Blessed are you who are poor, for yours is the kingdom of God")

Reversed position:

- Feeling of coming out of crises; finding resource and a stronghold (including in the spiritual sense)
- Recognition of own problems and attempt to overcome psychological limitations, connected to dissatisfaction and deficit

SIX OF PENTACLES

Harmony between "to give" and "to take"

Six of Pentacles represents the principle of providing and receiving resources. This is a new skill in the cycle of the suit development: not just to produce and accumulate something tangible (as it was on Three and Four of Pentacles), but rather to invest it, to provide and receive thanks to social interactions (and not direct-labor efforts). Here the relations of fair and harmonious exchange become a resource, just like "social capital"—which makes the suit deeper and more powerful. The esoteric card says that only balanced relations between two poles can lead to development. As soon as any source is underestimated and suppressed, the whole structure loses balance. The same thing happens with the inner psychic: when we are brave enough to look into the most-deprived corners of our consciousness (hence, the poorest and in the most need) and to share with them our currency of psychic vitality, we restore harmony and balance between the parts of our psyche. When being generous, showing magnanimity and compassion, and letting the energy freely circulate, we gain access to the abundancy of the whole Universe and development of our own personality.

Upright position:

- Inflow of a material resource; readiness to share its excesses to achieve fair balance; appearance of a benefactor
- Understanding feelings and needs of other people; openness, honesty, generosity
- A satisfying, sustainable decision

Reversed position:

- Disharmonious exchange (material, energetic, etc.), a shortfall on what is due; unfair distribution
- A resource that needs to be begged for; unpleasant dependency on other person's resource, rejection of help
- Sunk debts, overdue credits
- Egoism; ignoring of the necessities of a partner; "one has all the dues and the other—all the rights"

SEVEN OF PENTACLES

Patient cultivation with a postponed result

The soil has been processed and its internal resources have been used. We wait for seedlings, but Seven of Pentacles reminds us that everything has its pace. Attempts to speed up the normal cycle of development often lead to the opposite result—decrease in productivity. That's why the first meaning of Seven of Pentacles is futile investments. The second meaning: a flow of some process inspiring hope, which hasn't reached its finish yet and will require additional efforts and investments. Seven of Pentacles can be the Arcanum of profits received as a reward for work and patience. Are we ready to wait for the fruits to ripen? This card denies quick results allowing a person to move on. Attempts to do everything at the same time or at a record pace are useful. We are on a road. This road will go on for a very long time.

Upright position:
- Work, investment of efforts and means; care, cultivation
- Patience, long ripening; necessity to wait; postponed result
- Our attitude toward work, the result of which is hard to predict; a sober assessment of perspectives

Reversed position:
- Unsuccessful investments
- Difficulties, protractions
- Impatience and rush, leading to losses
- Tiredness, disappointment, dissatisfaction with the results from invested efforts

EIGHT OF PENTACLES

Royal mastery

In the material world, behind every success there is consistency, self-discipline, and attention to details. Eight of Pentacles informs us that it's all in our hands and everything goes right. Skillful, masterful, and very thorough work—these are typical meanings of this card. Eight of Pentacles is the Arcanum of mature professionalism, compulsory attitudes, skillfulness and inspiration in work, autonomy, and independence. Under pressure of circumstances, we often become impatient and act recklessly—but Eight of Pentacles does not know such problems. It knows what to focus on and what to ignore. It knows when to turn on the workaholic mode and when the most efficient activity is doing nothing. Work with the material under this card, which is perceived on the highest octave—as Alchemy. On all existence levels, abilities and opportunities that were long hidden become visible—the reflection of the ability to see the divine Spirit in the material.

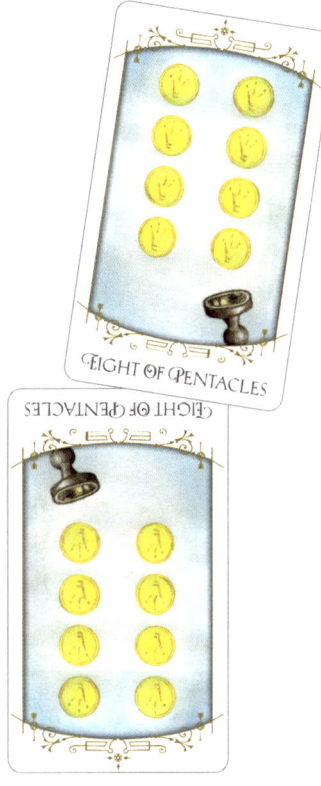

Upright position:

- Diligence, discipline, method, accuracy; high quality and well-thought-out performance of the work
- A well-established system with a potential for development, able to adapt for the tasks
- Repeated result; established conveyor work;
- Practice, repetition

Reversed position:

- Bad-quality work; problems with repeating results; delays, standstill
- Lack of attention to details; insufficient mastery or motivation; impatience
- Breach of instructions, requirements provisions
- Routine, boredom; tiredness from work

NINE OF PENTACLES

Exquisite success and prudent self-sufficiency

Nine of Pentacles is a clever approach to any good in your life, and the ability to disperse that good in the best way possible. It is a pleasure—but not one from indulgences, but rather from work well done and the organization of one's own life. It is not a joyful carelessness, but prudence, stability, regularity of life, and a confident position. This Arcanum has the talent to quickly turn any fortunate moments to its advantage. The beauty of Nine of Pentacles comes from the result of investments and work, expensive treatments, care, and procedures. She can dress well, have excellent taste, and emit around herself an aura of prosperity, even if with a hint of some solitude. The mind persuades itself that peace can be obtained through physical well-being and financial guarantees—spiritual interests withdraw to the second plan.

Upright position:

- Flourishing, prosperity, deserved fruits of labor, affluence; physical and financial well-being
- Common sense; confidence
- Stability, security
- Self-sufficiency, independence, autonomy, endowment; comfort solitude

Reversed position:

- Material losses; loss of stability; absence of discipline and life order in professional and financial affairs; financial dependency
- Feeling of being trapped, "golden cage," "monotonous happy life"; aspiration to break free
- Self-sufficiency and independence are no longer valued; solitude becomes a problem

TEN OF PENTACLES

Stable, smooth, well=established position—inside a steady and robust system

Ten of Pentacles reflects a culmination of expression of the qualities that belong to this suit. The Arcanum means that we are satisfied with ourselves and what is going on in our lives—where everything is literally in its place. Ten of Pentacles symbolizes the intention to create timeless values. This aspiration for "creative stability" is expressed in the need to put down roots, to build a house, to raise a family, or to have a sustainable career. Ten of Pentacles says that something valuable has been created, something that will withstand the test of time. We understand the price of what we own, and sense material, spiritual, and emotional satisfaction. This card indicates that we can rely on the support of our family (or that steady system we "installed into") and can provide support to others. Sometimes Ten of Pentacles predicts inheritance, both in a direct and indirect sense, when we talk about spiritual heritage. But we must remember: there is a new level in front of us. What has been achieved is significant and long term, but we shall see new opportunities to start new projects (Ace of Wands) behind it. Their absence will mean stagnation.

Upright position:

- Organic integration into system (family, kin, clan, corporation); feeling oneself to be a part of the whole; privileges, support from the system
- Family values and traditions; faithfulness to the roots; inheritance and assets
- Internal fulfillment and satisfaction; well-being
- Robust position; social and family stability

Reversed position:

- Intention to leave the system (family, clan, collective, company, etc.); wish for independence; negation of traditions and bonds; family problems
- Financial losses; loss of habitual stability
- Problems with assets or inheritance

Court Cards

Pages, Knights, Queens, and Kings

Pages

- Chance, opportunity for the principle of the suit to reveal itself

- Interest, impulse, "itch"

- Will to learn and progress

- Childish model of behavior and reactions

- News, word

- Initial stage of a process

- A significator of a child or an adolescent

PAGE OF WANDS

PAGE OF CUPS

PAGE OF SWORDS

PAGE OF PENTACLES

Page of Wands

A prompting impulse. Spontaneous creative rush. Desire to "play."

Pages present chances. A chance unfolding here has a form of some alluring idea or an offer—accepted by us with delight. With a fervent Page of Wands, it is an opportunity to step out of the usual sphere of interests, an invitation for an adventure, requiring courage and intention to take a risk, a bright brush amid the gray of every day. It can be, for example, participation in a contest, a sports competition, or any other opportunity to try one's strength; some unusual emotions, a small "discovery of America." It is a period of creativity, changes, a spontaneous beginning of something new, or an exciting anticipation of something. This card can suggest to await an outer impetus, some "hot news," important information, or a fascinating offer that can affect the conceived plan and can wake up a new willingness to act. Still, whether it will remain just a game or will work out into something serious, it is unclear. Pages are a minor rank of the figured Arcana, and they often lack maturity and responsibility.

Upright position:
- An inspiring idea or suggestion
- Desire to play, discover something new
- Curiosity, enthusiasm, ardency, spontaneity, honesty, desire for adventures
- A surprise, a new hobby
- Meaningful result is yet to come, but there is an interest and a willingness to try

Reversed position:
- Absence of interest or enthusiasm, reluctance for the new
- Unwillingness to learn and progress; lack of concentration; amateurism
- An unused chance
- Adventurism, childish pranks

Page of Cups

A romantic impulse. Dreams and reveries.

Page of Cups discovers the experience of intuitive-sensual perception of the world—through one's own experiences and sensations and the eternal "now." He serves the kingdom of emotions and relations and proclaims some events or chances in this field. As a rule, it is something pleasant—fresh feelings, new acquaintances, or fascination or obsession with something or somebody. It can be something new—even in current relations—a gift, a love confession. Page of Cups can indicate that an alluring invitation or a sincere compliment is on its way; somebody may show apparent friendliness or interest in you. But Page of Cups is not ready for depths of relations or dramatism; he is too young and volatile for that. This Arcanum represents the state of an easy exaltation, a passion for what satisfies the actual (and transitory) emotional needs, for example, with new music, a book, or a person. He is romantic, compassionate, sociable, and charismatic, but at the same time, naive and vulnerable, looks like a sensitive, loving and gifted, with a rich childlike imagination.

Upright position:

- Falling in love; demonstration of sincere feelings, flirt; a pleasant invitation
- Subtlety, sensitiveness, openness, trust, susceptibility, vulnerability
- Inspiration; follow inner images (dreams, reveries)
- Idealization; avoidance of conflicts and collisions; dependence on other people's opinions, ready to be led
- Aesthetics; birth of beauty (style, decorum, fashion, visage, etc.)

Reversed position:

- End of a quick love affair (with somebody or something)
- Excessive infantilism, hysteria, capriciousness; lack of self-reliance; dependence on another ("Parent")
- Emotional childhood trauma; hypersensitivity

Page of Swords
Impulse of analysis. Critical mind. Newborn thought.

Like air, the Swords are clear and uncompromising, manifesting in the Page of Swords primarily with mental perception of the world, intellect, and comprehension. This Page is concentrated on obtaining and analyzing information. It is an exclusive integrity and ideal of word and verbatim, norms and rules, oriented to practical use of intellect and rationality. The critical mind is activated. The reverse side of the energy of Page of Swords is a childish maximalism in relations with the others—coldness, direct clarification of a situation, and tough feedback without sentiments and adjustments to resentment of vis-à-vis.

Upright position:
- Dynamic exchange of information bits; seeking and checking of facts; quick mind and logic; new ideas
- Wariness, watchfulness, readiness to fight off an attack, surviving in a new environment ("an intern in a crisis department")
- Critics, quips, wits, cynicism
- Tangible result is not there so far, but there's interest and a willingness to try

Reversed position:
- A destructive and inappropriate model of behavior; acrimony, aggression, boycotts, laughing out, trolling, unethical behavior
- Open conflicts and confrontations
- Cracked personal mail, reading of other people's messages, ill-intentioned espionage
- Problems with communication and understanding each other

Page of Pentacles
Finding practical skills

Page of Pentacles represents experiments and experience on transformation of a matter through practical skill, primarily related to physical work: literally, what shall be done and in what consequence. The Arcanum encourages hard work, diligence, and serious attitude toward one's business and ideas. Page of Pentacles is a pupil, careful and realistic. He plans, calculates, evaluates, weighs, takes advice, and, after that, starts. And even if the result hasn't been reached yet—the potential is definitely there. This Page knows it well: not a single harmonizing and creative work will be wasted in the Universe, as there is no such thing as futile work. Even if it turned out to lack proper results from the point of view of the outer reality, it sharpened some appropriate edges in a person's soul.

Upright position:

- Intention to create and construct; finding practical skills, studies; pupil's position
- Hard work, zeal, commitment, persistence; an accurate approach; concentration on performed work
- Thorough study of an object or a question; attention to practical side of a question (in a broad sense)
- Tangible result is yet to appear, but there is interest and intention to try

Reversed position:

- Destructive and inappropriate model of behavior: lack of required diligence and hard work, unwillingness to consider previous mistakes and improve situation; infantile protest and rebellion
- Desire to obtain everything at once without applying proper efforts
- Impracticality; inadequate evaluation of own abilities

Knights

- Abilities supported by actions based on the suit (tryout of directions, dare)

- Aspiration for the change; new approaches

- Activity, dynamics, journeys

- An energy of youth ("young kings"); some physical entity not having, as a rule, any significant status or power in the current situation, but remaining active and proactive based on the principle of the suit

KNIGHT OF WANDS

KNIGHT OF CUPS

KNIGHT OF SWORDS

KNIGHT OF PENTACLES

Knight of Wands

Appetite for deeds and achievements

Knight of Wands is full of strength, youth, and energy; he outpours aggression, health, and willingness for activities, hunting, and adventures. It is a dynamic principle of the suit of Wands: he is concentrated on himself and his desires, needs, and motives; hence self-admiration, self-proclaim. Knight of Wands is a bright and notable person, committed to his idea. His appearance brings a flash of enthusiasm, an infusion of fresh forces. Energy, initiative, readiness to act, a spirit of a pioneer. His environment is excitement, impulsiveness, and spontaneity. If he did appear, it means he's ready to strike. The main strength of Knight of Wands is determination to move forward (so that others could see that).

Upright position:

- Buoyant activity for some global task; "storm and onslaught"; a flow of events, dynamics; options—options—options
- Passion, impatience, impulsiveness, excitement, lust for life, enthusiasm, scrappy behavior; "a cowboy"
- There are some midstage (not final, not stable) results, but what's more important is that there is an animated sparkling activity, aimed to achieve those results

---

Reversed position:

- Foolishness, amateurism, impatience, recklessness and indiscretion; discord and dissonance; rash, impulsive actions ("to jump head over heels")
- Bad temper, aggressiveness
- Problems with utilization of sexual energy
- Boiling energy accumulates but has no creative outcome; a process loses its effective dynamics; a result is not achieved

Knight of Cups

Enamored stranger

Knight of Cups, like Page of Cups, relies on feelings, but differently from the latter; it is utterly important for this Knight to have a constant object of his feelings. It can be a beautiful sensation or an image-inducing amazing emotion ("I'm in love with the Love itself"). Knight of Cups represents a head-in-the-clouds Grail seeker, worshipping the eternal feminine aspect of God. On a deep psychological level, this Knight rejoins the archetypic energies of the male and the female. This Arcanum describes a pleasant atmosphere, filled with benevolence, cordiality, and warmth; here romantic acquaintances form, dates are proposed, and visiting places where meetings of emotionally gifted people interested in each other frequent. All that resembles an opportunity for a new love. Knight of Cups is a wonderful lover, rather in the old-fashioned way than in the modern one. He is a lover not for the brilliance of skin, but for the bloom of the soul. He is instinctively perceived by a woman as a gift, a psychological salvation—and his appearance can produce a truly hypnotic impact on her. Even if he turns out to be gay.

Upright position:

- "An image of a new love" (in relationships, work, hobbies, or friendship), pleasant proposals and opportunities; initiation of friendly or romantic contacts; emotionally enriched connection with a creative, dreamy person of group of people (here the accent is not on a person but rather on a state)
- Benevolence, peacefulness, compassion, understanding; expression of feelings, emotional emancipation
- Inclination to idealize
- An "atmospheric" event (a date, a party, a theater, etc.)

Reversed position:

- Manipulation of feelings, "betrayed love"; malevolent creation of illusions, deceit, treachery, mischief
- Hypersensitivity, capture by images; "pink glasses"
- Emotional disbalance, depression; an attempt to leave an exhausting emotional situation
- Dependencies (drugs, alcohol, etc.)

Knight of Swords

Rule and principle put up to a cult. Fierce opposition.

Knight of Swords almost always marks dramatically developing stress situations, getting into the center of some upheavals. Its appearance means that somebody is burning with an idea. Knight of Swords has his own reality in which he is totally sure of himself: it is an unbreakable belief in own rightness that can quickly turn into a righteous anger and a rapid attack head over heels on those who disagree. Knight of Swords is a chill of alienation, sharp discussions, harsh disagreement, evil tongue, and acrid irony. That's why Knight of Swords often foreshadows a quarrel, breakup, fierce polemics, and sometimes even open aggression. In his supervision are sharp conflicts and fights. Gloomy and evil determination, bitter mindset, audacity, desperation, pressure, ability to show teeth, and a blatant shortsightedness. Nevertheless, in upright position this card always points at a high intellectual potential, which can be used in peaceful purposes as well. Sometimes the card signifies a phenomenal ingenuity, quick wit, and ability to do thousands of things in a bit of time. Knight of Swords is also good at providing strength to resist somebody or something; he has a belief in his own right, and a fearless will to defeat some "monster."

Upright position:

- Sharp conflict situation, an aggressive dispute, sharp criticisms, quarrel, right up to breakup; an impulse "to find and punish the enemy," even immediately; polemics (including internal dialogues cracking the head)
- Wildness, conflicts, cynicism, indiscretion; fanatically lured by some idea
- Quick reaction, rapidity, velocity; business trips and journeys (quick and stressful)
- Ability to quickly react and act in a crisis situation; ability to act heroically

---

Reversed position:

- Radical impulsive acts, turning back on the initiator; aggression, ruthlessness and vindictiveness; threats and violence; loss of control; disruption
- Ridiculous and illogical accusations; "fight with windmills"
- Traumas, fractures, crashes; problems with trips and during them

Knight of Pentacles

Small strokes fell great oaks.

When a Knight of Pentacles appears, then something useful is going to take place—something that will yield benefits. It symbolizes material aspirations, diligence, and a will for stability and reliability. This is the most conservative and slow of all the Knights, the most meticulous and steady. He brings the impulse of conscientiousness, responsibility, and performance. Knight of Pentacles pays attention to details and is diligent and systematic; his perfectionism is purely specific, oriented toward confidence in proper quality of the work that he has done. Procrastination is not his problem: he urges to combat all kinds of laziness; he pulls himself together and carries his objective to results. As any of the Knights, he seeks and tries options, but inside a preassigned perimeter—this Knight stays away from risk.

Upright position:

- Useful, well-thought-out, methodical actions, aimed for a specific objective (financial gains, creative efforts, health improvement, relationships)
- Advantageous opportunities that shall be evaluated and considered; favorable circumstances
- Consistency, systematic approach, persistence, determination, order, practicality, realistic goal-setting; common sense; accountability
- Slow but steady movement

Reversed position:

- Apathy, inertia, laziness; loss of internal goal and enthusiasm
- Narrow-mindedness, rigidity
- Physical needs become the main and sole priority
- Process slows down; result hasn't been achieved

QUEENS

- A specific woman (a significator of a querent or women in his circle)

- Female model of behavior and reactions (one of the subpersonalities of a querent or other person who appears in the field of the setup)

- Mastery, practicality, competencies—based on the strengths of the suit

- Self-sufficiency—in the principle of the suit

- Custody, education, coaching—on the principle of the suit

- "Internal" guiding power

- A female archetype (4 Queens form the archetype of the Empress)

Queen of Wands

Queen of Cups

Queen of Swords

Queen of Pentacles

Queen of Wands
An actress on a social scene. A motivator and an inspirer.
"I can't fail to be liked."

Queen of Wands informs us that claims for leadership are now valid, and there is pride and ambition at stake. This card always sensitively responds to ambitions, aspiration for independence and autonomy, professional and social success, and personal growth. The reality of Queen of Wands is social interactions and social roles; she—as all members of the suit of Wands—is oriented toward them. That's why it's important to her what is being said about her. This Queen knows how to get what she wants through understanding motives of others. She knows how to "get deals." With the same likelihood, she will use her power or status along with her high energy, personal charisma, and sexual attractiveness. Queen of Wands is excellent at sensing power and influencing others; she will try either to adjust to such a person to get her bonuses and part of the influence or instead will compete and try to eliminate him on the social field. Queen of Wands can have a hard time staying near a strong man because she competes with him, but she has the same hard time with a weak man because of a lack of respect. Still . . . it is Queen of Wands who can motivate her man for achievements unlike any other, fanning the flames of ambitions in him.

UPRIGHT POSITION:
- A woman—extraverted, charismatic, sexual, assured, ambitious, inspiring, independent
- Recognition on a social scene; desire to be the center of attention; brilliance, expression, originality, an artistic talent; high self-esteem
- Self-realization, ambitions, resourcefulness, energy
- Well-developed social intellect; talent to acquire useful connections
- A constructive process, contributing to social elevation

REVERSED POSITION:
- A destructive or improper model of behavior; female archetype of a competitor, a rival, a seducer; "a schemer-bitch," an energetic psychopath; a woman inclined to hysterical, impulsive reactions, not understanding what she really does want
- An improper provocative behavior
- Arrogance, vindictiveness, wrathfulness (extraverted negative emotionality)
- Intrigues and manipulations, gossip
- Painfully hurt ambitions with respective consequences
- A process is not developing or is developing in a perverted format

Queen of Cups
A good sorceress "out of this world"

Queen of Cups is the most susceptible Queen, and she is limitlessly feminine. Symbolically, it's water that takes the form of any vessel; this Queen can become a filling inspiration for any man and can turn her own life into a masterpiece. Queen of Cups lives in a world of sensations, impressions, visions, and fantasies—her deep emotional perception becomes her main criterion to define the world. What she feels is the truth; she dwells in numerous reflections of reality, created by herself. Sensitivity of Queen of Cups makes her very attractive, although a bit "not from around here." She is always partly in an "elves' world" and hence can often be distracted and not very practical. But her intuition exceeds all expectations. Queen of Cups is a fairy and an oracle, interpreting dreams; a psychic helping to find a way in a haze. She is a muse who intuitively feels what talents and abilities are there in a person standing next to her. Her gifts are precious insights.

Upright position:

- A woman—tender, kind, attentive, understanding, trusting her feelings, intuitive, who has an excellent contact with her subconscious, dreamy, delicate; irrational, not very practical
- Support, care, understanding; close healing contact; power of empathy
- Deep insights; a touch upon hidden feelings, revelation of the innermost
- Intuition, provision; meditation, spiritual practices
- A process is evolving according to a mood and an internal state

Reversed position:

- A destructive inappropriate model of behavior; unstable psychic state, withdrawal to the world of illusions, unfounded fears, anxiety, depression; inclination to hysteria and manipulations; excess vulnerability and resentment
- Codependent relations; total merge with the object of one's desires
- Dependencies (alcohol, drugs, sex; food addictions)
- Weak will; passivity

QUEEN OF SWORDS
Merciless professional

Queen of Swords represents the space of mental control, both internal (self-organization, elimination of contradictions, discipline) and external (practical implementation of laws and rules). Her absolute self-confidence can be scary; nevertheless, she always expresses her thoughts in a direct and open manner, decisively cuts off the redundant, and sees the very core of a situation. She postulates the truth and principles independently of what other people feel about it. Queen of Swords often helps others with wise advice, but sometimes it's hard to comply with her perfectionist standards. She doesn't promise an easy and quick result—the business is going, but within protocols in force and in strict accordance with established rules. It is a woman's expression of the air element, putting on a difficult task: integration of mind and feelings. Queen of Swords shall learn to accept her own emotions and feelings, not cutting them off with her shiny sword.

UPRIGHT POSITION:

- A woman—intellectual, with a critical mind, unprejudiced, objective, competent, strict, independent, incorruptible, certain of her rightness (justified), emotionally cold, suspicious
- Well-considered actions, complying with the rules and established standards; a process is constructively developing under tight rational management, based on logic and objectivity; competence and professionalism
- Wise advice based on experience, observations, and analysis; elimination of contradictions, "to sort out the details"; objective unemotional critics

REVERSED POSITION:

- Destructive inappropriate model of behavior; sharp temper; excessive criticism; perfectionism and suspiciousness; overcontrol
- Severe grudge and desire to revenge; "I won't ever forgive you for that!"; disappointment in intimacy and love; negation of feelings; "freeze"
- Narrow-mindedness, rigidity, scant outlook; getting stuck in the model of her own correctness, and "only this way and never any other"
- Hypocrisy, false morale
- Solitude, depression, autoaggression; an important attribute of the reversed Queen of Swords is lack of something; it is a person acting not from excess, but driven by deficiency, shortage of what is vital (hence, probably a sharp temper?)

Queen of Pentacles
Mother of a big family.

Queen of Pentacles is not the one in need. She is a woman of means, used to enjoying affluence and comfort, with money and wealth. Her sphere is a secure and stable material reality with such attributes as a solid career, income, robust marriage, and house, and a pension plan on top of that. She strongly connects us to the world around, its worries, and all the pleasant things it has to offer; she has roots in "simple earthly delights." Queen of Pentacles indicates that we have plenty to take care of: shopping, house, family, tidying up, and the creation of a cozy comfortable environment. She pragmatically takes care of the resources and their preservation, nourishes interest in business, nature, animals, household, questions of well-being, interior, and landscape designs. Sensuality of Queen of Pentacles is always colored in a mother's tones. Taking advantage of her common sense and intrinsic sensory features, she helps bloom and bear fruits to everything around in her charge.

Upright position:
- A woman—practical, reasonable, effective, wealthy, hospitable and thrifty; taking care of material well-being, comfort, and health
- Home and coziness; care and kindness; "warm and well fed"
- Decorative and applied arts
- Maturity and sensuality; bloom and fruit bearing; motherhood
- Accumulation and multiplication of resources; a process is developing well, thanks to wise and practical control and maternal energy

Reversed position:
- A destructive and inappropriate model of behavior; lack of practicality, disorder, loose care of material resources; inefficient resource management (splurge or clutter), proprietary behavior (including toward people, children)
- Loss of stability, threat to material or physical prosperity; energy exhaustion; infertility
- Lack of mastery or competencies; a process is stagnating or developing pointlessly and unprofessionally

Kings

- A specific man (a significator or a querent or men in his circle)

- Male model of behavior and reactions (one of subpersonalities of a querent or other person who appears in the field of the setup)

- Full mastery of the principle of the suit; outer (visible) power, authority, and expertise (based on the principle of the suit); system management in a vertical regime complying hierarchies and delegating

- Making decisions and readiness to take responsibility

- Tangible result; sustainable group unity with a common goal and ideology (company, enterprise, team, party, club, social group, etc.)

- Male archetype (4 Kings form the archetype of the Emperor)

KING OF WANDS

KING OF CUPS

KING OF SWORDS

KING OF PENTACLES

King of Wands

Energetic involving leadership. Blossom of social realization, power, and achievements. "Said and done."

King of Wands enjoys a kind of theatrical gesture and an orchestra upon his arrival: entourage, encirclement, observers, adoring crowd. Then he is ready for generous articulate gestures, especially in breach of formalities. He likes it; this is his way to bend the rules of this world to suit him. Leadership qualities, will, lust for life, and passion—these are the main traits of King of Wands. Manhood, ownership, and responsibility are attached. This card is also associated with firm position, dignity, and strength—and readiness to protect those accepted in the family. King of Wands is able to inspire others, instilling tremendously large-scale ideas in them. He is a sharp strategist, but these are inspired and creative strategies in contrast to precise calculation. This King possesses an excellent intuition and is capable of inspiring and leading many, literally in the flow of his libido. He is highly productive and energetic. The achieved does not satisfy him; he aims for more, for he is afraid that without aspiring for more, he will lose what he has already. When a battle in his life is over, he immediately starts a new one.

Upright position:
- A man—a leader, charismatic, manly, assured, socially established, generous, magnanimous; "I won't let you hurt my friends"; an outstanding organizer, a businessman, a politician, a manager, a person with a high social position; somewhat egocentric and dependent on his entourage
- A principle of power; a fulfilling free will; a decisive, responsible, and well-thought-out action
- Achieving a sound and socially meaningful result; a cheerful management of a system (a company, a collective, a family, etc.)

Reversed position:
- A destructive or inappropriate model of behavior; arrogance, hubris, stubbornness, aggressive autocracy; "hollow macho" and "naked king" (a lot of screams and impulsive actions to show off)
- Hidden infantilism and problems with manly self-esteem; an ideal object for manipulations
- Problems with effectiveness of management, loss of power and control; a system suffering from poor management; a result is not reached or is eroded
- Renunciation from a leading role; "to step down"

King of Cups

Psychologically integrated leader. Empathetic leadership and mentorship.

King of Cups possesses an intuitive wisdom, a great knowledge of a human nature, and, at the same time, a calm and lenient attitude toward others' flaws (which to King of Swords seems impossible). He represents inner voice, which gives ethical evaluation of what is happening and guiding us to the right path. He is a benefactor ready to listen and to facilitate. Delicacy and liberal behavior are inherent to him; often he is quite a powerful personality with a bright individuality, internally developed and noble to the point unavailable for others. Disadvantages of this King: an inclination to passive resistance and self-deceit instead of a direct "no" (it's hard for him to deny something to somebody), lack of resilience for stress, and tough adaptation to life's realities. This Arcanum talks about implementation of creative talents and intuition for development of one's own career. Wisdom, diplomacy, and ability to provide support, having evaluated the environment in the right way, can become a successful way for self-realization (priest, advocate, family doctor, occult mentor, life coach, facilitator, or psychologist). King of Cups has high sensitivity and a good imagination; these qualities can be very useful in artistic studies. Also he represents the archetype of the "wounded healer," trying to heal his pain by helping others. He has the advanced ability to empathize and sympathize, to tune in to another person and be an intuitive adviser. In the center of his interest, there will always be a human. King of Cups aims to create emotional bonds more than any other King, although he usually hides his emotions well. Interaction with people stimulates him for a hidden psychological leadership.

Upright position:

- A man—a leader, benevolent, sophisticated, empathetic, diplomatic, sympathizing, helping, magnanimous, caring
- Maturity and experience in the questions of relationships; good, wise advice; consultation, consolation, spiritual vision, intuitive understanding
- Creative approach to management, stimulation of a human potential development
- A business or a company "according to what the heart wants"

Reversed position:

- Destructive or inappropriate model of behavior; shocking, eccentric behavior; mood ups and downs, passive aggression
- Egoism, ethical manipulation; to live on account of another; a talented extortionist (for instance, marriage crook)
- Psycho-emotional disorders; dependent narcissism
- Deceit and self-deceit
- Addiction to alcohol, drugs, etc.

King of Swords

"I am the law and the system." Authoritarian leadership with punishment of disobedient.

King of Swords is a symbol of a common, strict, semimilitary organization with purely regulated subordination, mandate, and functions. He represents a harsh director, the head of some hierarchy. And here it is important to decide—is law above him? Or is he the law himself? If the second, then it is strongly not recommended to stay within his system, because it can cause arbitrariness. King of Swords is a social structure oriented to test "danger safety," the state of public organism (what intelligence services of different countries do), and services of the correction of vices and execution of punishments (penitentiary system). King of Swords has a ruthless ability to make decisions, trying to always be supereffective and precise in everything he does. He can act as peacemaker as well, but again from the position of power. Composure, critical approach, and, importantly, precise realization of own decisions. King of Swords is a strong man: authoritative, powerful, accustomed to give orders and observe obedience, enforcing his decisions, sometimes excessively cruel and relentless but still thinking logically. His distinctive trait is that he always counts more on himself than on others. He combines remarkable prudence and, not least, remarkable fearlessness.

UPRIGHT POSITION:

- A man—tough leader, strong, powerful, authoritative, ruthless, principled, prudent, direct, "arbiter of truth"; a man "in the exercise," a judge, a military person, a representative of the executive power, a surgeon, a critic, an inspector
- Interaction with a system (a "strictly regulated" organization, inspecting, supervising, and law-enforcing organs and other regulators); control and inspection
- Critical thinking, logic, strategic calculation, intolerance of mistakes and disobedience
- Fearlessness, self-discipline, self-control

REVERSED POSITION:

- A destructive or inappropriate model of behavior; cruelty, dictatorship, arbitrariness, suspiciousness, vindictiveness, destructive and radical decisions; inhumanity, "the ends justify the means"
- A collision with a representative of authority with a negative outcome (for example, an unfair and excessive punishment, threats); problems with the law; actions against the law
- An opponent fighting dirty; a loss; a conflict

King of Pentacles
A wealthy patriarch.

The imposing and respectable King of Pentacles possesses the great gift of turning his efforts into material wealth and values, controlling construction of his civilization. He is an acknowledged leader with massive life experience behind him, a member of business and financial circles, and a successful entrepreneur. King of Pentacles can provide real support and give wise advice. He is firmly on his feet, and everything that he creates is solid and steady. This figure is either indifferent or benevolent to a querent, but never hostile. As with all the Kings, he represents a competent and serious approach and responsible attitudes. King of Pentacles possesses the blessing of the mythical King of Midas: whatever he touches grows and flourishes—until it's a material world. There is something of a bull in him—not only in terms of qualities related to the Earthly sign of Taurus, but also in terms of optimism and confidence in that everything is for the better. King of Pentacles is a very "Earthly" king: steady, pragmatic, brutal, and lascivious. Though a provider and patriarch, sometimes he considers people as property or valuables.

Upright position:
- A man—respectable, imposing, steady, experienced, practical, reliable, reasonable, conservative, substantial, resilient; a patriarch, protecting family and family values; a banker or a businessman, managing financial flows
- Financial stability, "a robust base"; confident, expanding, and nonrisky entrepreneurship; obtaining material goods
- Practical help, experience, and competency
- Comfort, hedonism; lust for life with its physical pleasures
- Obtaining a robust result; high quality

Reversed position:
- A destructive, inappropriate model of behavior; greed, fixation on material side of a question, rude or vulgar behavior, "brutality" in its negative sense; jealousy, envy; narrow-mindeness
- Exploitation of people, resources, nature, etc.— for material profit; "dirty" means
- Material losses, financial destabilization, degradation of well-being; inability to manage
- Lust and gluttony; excesses in physical desires
- Result hasn't been reached or its quality is unsatisfactor

Conclusion

Practicing Tarot is always an encounter: either with oneself or a helper (a tarologist) and a querent (asking for help). Every one of us comes into such contact as we are, with our own life experience, with traumas, ancestors, and stories behind them. It requires a great deal of acceptance; openness to what shall be revealed without steady concepts, expectations, or rules.

We all live in our own world and have our own subjective visions of it. Through a reading we inevitably project our model of world, which may not reflect the model of a client. It is important though to remember that an observer affects what is observed, and a reader, bringing his/her own interpretations, modifies readings and the information field around it. Such interference cannot be avoided, but we can rely on the idea that this particular client came to us for a reason. And, of course, on the wisdom of that Indefinite Ubiquity we call collective unconscious or universal soul, or God . . . something we all are a part of—

The one who knows the divine plan and loves us indefinitely.

About the Author

STANISLAV RESHETNIKOV was born and lives in Moscow, Russia. He's a graduate of Moscow Medical Academy with a specialization in pharmacology and pharmaceutical marketing. After years of successful work as a marketer for big-pharma companies and reaching top positions in business, he shifted his focus to the psychology and surrounding disciplines, especially the Jungian school. This way led to completion of the Moscow association of analytical psychology (Jungian analysis). Stanislav became a skilled tarologist, psychotherapist, trainer, and leader of several popular thematic seminars and created his own course on Tarot learning, based on years of practical experience and numerous cases.

To contact the author,
email: stan.reshetnikov@gmail.com